An indispensable guide for every home, IN CASE OF EMERGENCY contains concise, authoritative instructions for emergency care for sudden illnesses and accidents—the recommended steps for proper care and relief until the doctor comes.

> What situations you can handle yourself—and exactly how to handle them.

> What situations are dangerous and require a doctor's help.

> What situations are so dangerous there's no time for a doctor—and what to do then.

Clear, simple, well-illustrated instructions . . . everything from treating a bullet wound or delivering a baby to stopping a nose bleed or getting a bug out of your ear.

> "A solid tome of authoritative advice to help you meet every conceivable accident or illness."—*Good Housekeeping*

> "Highly recommended"—*Library Journal*

EMERGENCY TELEPHONE NUMBERS

FAMILY DOCTOR _____ PHONE_____

ADDRESS _____

PEDIATRICIAN _____ PHONE_____

ADDRESS _____

OBSTETRICIAN _____ PHONE_____

ADDRESS _____

EYE DOCTOR _____ PHONE_____

ADDRESS _____

POISON CONTROL CENTER _____ PHONE_____

ADDRESS _____

DENTIST _____ PHONE_____

ADDRESS _____

OCULIST _____ PHONE_____

ADDRESS _____

AMBULANCE _____ PHONE_____

ADDRESS _____

HOSPITAL _____ PHONE_____

ADDRESS _____

HOSPITAL _____ PHONE_____

ADDRESS _____

POLICE _____ PHONE_____

FIRE DEPARTMENT _____ PHONE_____

DRUG STORE (ALL NIGHT) _____ PHONE_____

ADDRESS _____

DRUG STORE (NEIGHBORHOOD) _____ PHONE_____

ADDRESS _____

BUSINESS _____ PHONE_____

NEIGHBOR _____ PHONE_____

NEIGHBOR _____ PHONE_____

RELATIVE _____ PHONE_____

RELATIVE _____ PHONE_____

QUICK-INDEX

IN CASE OF EMERGENCY

What to Do Until the Doctor Arrives

BRY BENJAMIN, M.D.

and

ANNETTE FRANCIS BENJAMIN

Illustrated by MARTA CONE

PYRAMID BOOKS   NEW YORK

IN CASE OF EMERGENCY

A PYRAMID BOOK
Published by arrangement with Doubleday & Company, Inc.

Doubleday edition published August, 1965
Pyramid edition published April, 1967

Library of Congress catalog card number 65-15661

Printed in the United States of America

PYRAMID BOOKS are published by Pyramid Publications, Inc.,
444 Madison Avenue, New York, New York 10022, U.S.A.

FOREWORD

When a member of your family suddenly becomes ill or has an accident at home, *prompt and proper emergency care* can make the difference between life and death. *This book tells you what to do.*

Sometimes there are things you should or must do *even before calling the doctor. After you reach the doctor* this book will help you to follow his instructions. It will also go a long way toward relieving the pain, anxiety, fright, and feeling of helplessness which accompany emergency situations.

To get the most out of this book, familiarize yourself with its contents. Note where and how you can find what you want to find in a hurry. *There is a Quick Index inside the front cover for emergency use,* and the first section of the book contains detailed instructions for use in life-threatening situations.

Practice such *techniques* as mouth-to-mouth breathing, locating pressure points, finding and counting a pulse, and carrying another person. Then you will be much more effective and confident if you should find you have to use them.

In the great majority of situations discussed in this book, we have advised you to call your doctor. In each specific situation we have advised you *when* your doctor should be called, for there will be times when you must carry out some initial measure as we have indicated—even before calling your doctor.

Wherever emergencies are preventable, as in the case of accidental poisoning and burns, we have listed basic and detailed *safety rules* which should become a permanent part of your everyday life. Careful *prevention* minimizes the chances that you and your family will ever have to face emergencies of this kind.

THE AUTHORS

ACKNOWLEDGMENTS

We wish to express grateful acknowledgment to the following sources for information and statistics generously supplied:

The American Medical Association
The United States Public Health Service
The American National Red Cross
The American Cancer Society
The Office of Civil Defense, United States Department of Defense
The Office of Naval Intelligence, United States Department of the Navy
The National Safety Council
The National Office of Vital Statistics
The American Society for the Prevention of Cruelty to Animals
The New York Diabetes Association
The New York City Department of Health, Poison Control Center
The New York City Fire Department

We would like to thank Miss Doris Lowe, Reference Librarian, Cornell University Medical College Library, and Stanley J. Behrman, D.D.S., Assistant Clinical Professor of Surgery, Cornell University Medical College, and Attending Oral Surgeon at the New York Hospital, for their valuable assistance.

CONTENTS

PART TWO—ACCIDENTS

PART FOUR—HEAD AND BRAIN INJURIES AND DISORDERS

PART FIVE—OTHER POTENTIALLY SERIOUS PROBLEMS

PART SIX—PSYCHIATRIC EMERGENCIES

PART SEVEN—DENTAL EMERGENCIES

PART EIGHT—HOME EMERGENCY SUPPLIES

EMERGENCY MEDICAL IDENTIFICATION SYMBOL

The symbol shown here was devised by the American Medical Association to signal that a victim of sudden illness or an accident may need special medical attention. It is increasing in world-wide use since its adoption in 1964 by the World Medical Association.

The victim may be carrying an identification card with vital information—or he may be wearing an identification bracelet or some other metal or plastic device containing the information on his ankle or around his neck.

If you find yourself in the situation of helping a person who is unconscious or dazed, look for such identification. The person may be a diabetic and need insulin in addition to treatment for possible injuries. This identification is also helpful for people with known allergies to certain drugs, those who need certain medicines, sufferers of epileptic seizures, and many others.

If you have any condition which might require special treatment in an emergency, you should consider carrying or wearing an emergency identification symbol which calls attention to it. Your doctor can advise you whether or not to use one, where to obtain it, and what to have written or engraved on it.

HOW TO GET MEDICAL HELP

Medical care cannot be dispensed by machine. It involves as personal a relationship and technique as exist in our society today. You must get to know your physician, and he must get to know you. So it is wisest to select a family or personal physician *when you are well.*

Most people will make their selection on the basis of personal knowledge or the recommendation of friends or relatives. If you are in a strange community, the local county medical society or nearest hospital will be able to help you with your choice.

Once having selected your doctor, arrange to meet him. During this first visit, whether you are well or ill, you should be sure to find out:

1. How you can reach him at all times.

2. What provisions he has made for your care when he is away.

3. What to do in an emergency situation in case he cannot be reached right away.

If you do not have a doctor—in case of emergency— a friend, neighbor, or passer-by can call his doctor to help you. If you are alone, telephone the police or the nearest hospital. Or tell the telephone operator what the trouble is, giving her your name, address, and telephone number. *Keep calm and make absolutely certain you have been clearly understood.*

In many communities throughout the United States there is a telephone listing of physicians under "Doctors' Emergency Service" or the local county medical society. In most towns the Yellow Pages directory usually contains a complete list of doctors' names under "Physicians."

17

Part One

LIFESAVING PROCEDURES

— 1 —

THE FIRST THINGS TO DO

IN CASE OF EMERGENCY

1. Keep the patient lying down, his head level with the rest of his body. In case of suspected head injuries, raise his head slightly.

2. Don't move him, unless absolutely necessary, as in case of fire. Splint any broken bones (pp. 77-79) before attempting to move him if there is time.

3. Make sure that air passages are open in any unconscious or injured person. If the airway is obstructed by food, mucus, blood, or vomitus, turn his head to one side. Wipe out the back of his throat with your finger, preferably wrapped in a handkerchief.

4. Make sure he is breathing. If he is not, tilt his head backward, pull his jaw forward, and begin mouth-to-mouth breathing (pp. 22-29).

5. Treat any serious external bleeding by applying pressure directly over the wound with sterile dressings or clean cloth until the bleeding stops (pp. 30-33). Do not hesitate to use **any** material or even your bare hand in an effort to stop the bleeding. If heavy bleeding is coming from a limb, elevate the limb above the level of the heart, unless you suspect a broken bone.

6. Don't give him anything by mouth if he is unconscious or semiconscious.

7. Cover him and keep him comfortably warm.

21

– 2 –

MOUTH-TO-MOUTH BREATHING

FOR ASPHYXIATION

(Rescue Breathing, Mouth-to-Mouth Resuscitation)

Mouth-to-mouth breathing is the use of a person's breath to revive someone who is unable to breathe for himself. Since death by asphyxiation claims approximately fifty thousand victims a year in the United States due to combined causes—drowning, electrocution, suffocation, choking, drug overdosage, carbon monoxide and smoke poisoning — it is important for everyone to be familiar with the means of restoring breath which means life itself.

Speed is essential, as even a ten-second delay can make the difference between life and death.

When to Use It

Begin mouth-to-mouth breathing **without delay—** if there is a third person present, have *him* call the doctor while *you* begin—if there is absence of any breathing movements or if the victim's lips, tongue or fingernails are bluish in color. When in doubt, begin mouth-to-mouth breathing. Absolutely no harm can come from its use and serious harm can come if its use is delayed.

Advantages Over Other Methods

The oldest method of resuscitation, mouth-to-mouth breathing has an interesting history. It has been practiced widely since antiquity to treat victims of asphyxia (from the Greek, meaning stoppage of the pulse, and therefore, stoppage of breathing). It is described in the Bible, II Kings, Chapter 4, Verse 34, and was the method of choice until the year 1530.

Following the sixteenth century other forms of artificial respiration began to be thought more suitable, because mouth-to-mouth breathing was considered vulgar. In recent years it has once again taken its place as the most effective method of treating asphyxiation.

Mouth-to-mouth breathing requires no special equipment. The victim does not need to be placed on the ground or in any special position. It can be given even when the victim is in the water in cases of drowning, or in cramped surroundings.

Mouth-to-mouth breathing can be maintained for **hours** without fatigue, even when the victim is twice the size of the rescuer. It is so simple that almost anyone, including a child, can learn it and use it effectively.

MOUTH-TO-MOUTH BREATHING FOR INFANTS AND SMALL CHILDREN

1. If there is any foreign matter (such as mucus, vomitus, chewing gum, food, sand) visible in the mouth, turn the child's head to one side. Wipe the mouth out quickly with your fingers or a handkerchief wrapped around your fingers—reaching far back into the throat, if necessary.

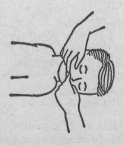

2. Put the child in face-up position.

3. Tilt the child's head backward until the skin over the throat is stretched.

4. Lift the child's chin or lower jaw forward with the fingers of both hands so that the jaw is jutting out, keeping the lips slightly open with your thumb.

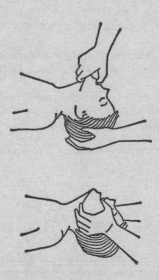

5. Keep the child in this position so that his tongue will not fall back to block the air passage.

6. *Open your mouth wide,* seal your lips around the child's MOUTH AND NOSE. (For an older child, if you cannot cover both nose and mouth, use mouth-to-

mouth preferably. If that is not possible, use mouth-to-nose.) You may place a handkerchief over the child's mouth and/or nose if you want to avoid direct contact.

7. Blow your breath gently into the child's mouth and nose until you see the chest rise and you feel the lungs expand.

8. Then remove your mouth and let the child breathe out.

9. As soon as you hear the breath come out, place your mouth over his mouth and nose, and repeat the procedure.

10. Repeat twenty times a minute—that is, every three seconds.

11. When possible, place your hand over the child's stomach, using moderate pressure to prevent the stomach from becoming filled with air.

12. Continue until the child begins to breathe for himself or until the physician arrives.

MOUTH-TO-MOUTH BREATHING
AND MOUTH-TO-NOSE BREATHING
FOR ADULT VICTIMS

The choice between mouth-to-mouth and mouth-to-nose breathing is not of great importance. Use whatever will work best. For example, mouth-to-nose breathing should be used if the victim is convulsing, if his mouth is difficult to open, or if his stomach fills up too much with air during mouth-to-mouth breathing. Use mouth-to-mouth breathing if the nasal passages are blocked.

1. If there is any foreign matter (such as mucus, vomitus, chewing gum, food, sand) visible in the mouth, turn the victim's head to one side. Wipe the mouth out quickly with your fingers or a handkerchief wrapped around your fingers—reaching far back into the throat, if necessary.

2. Put the victim in face-up position.

3. Lift the neck and tilt the head backward so that the skin over the throat is stretched. One hand should push the top of the head backward while the other hand pulls the chin or lower jaw forward.

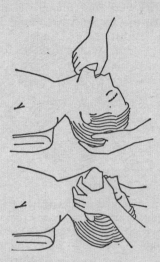

4. Take a deep breath. *Open your mouth wide* over the victim's mouth or nose. You may place a handkerchief over the person's mouth or nose if you want to avoid direct contact.

For mouth-to-mouth breathing:

Seal your lips widely around the victim's mouth. Fold his lower lip down to keep his mouth open. To prevent leakage of air out through the nose, either pinch the subject's nostrils with your thumb and finger or press your cheek against his nostrils during inflation.

For mouth-to-nose breathing:

Make a leakproof seal by placing your lips widely on the victim's cheeks around his nose (be sure your lips do not close or obstruct his nostrils). Keep and hold the victim's lips closed with your thumb.

5. Blow your breath vigorously into the victim until you see the chest rise. Then remove your mouth to let him breathe out.

6. Take your next breath as you listen to the sound of his breath escaping.

7. Reinflate his lungs again as soon as he has breathed out.

8. Repeat ten to fifteen times a minute—that is, every five or six seconds.

9. Gurgling or noisy breathing indicates the need to improve the head backward position—or to clear the throat again as in Step No. 1.

10. Continue rescue breathing until the person begins to breathe for himself or until the physician arrives.

Airway (or Resuscitation) Tube

You can easily obtain at your drugstore an inexpensive plastic tube which can be used to resuscitate adults and children over three years of age. One end is inserted *over* the victim's tongue—the other end serves as a mouthpiece for the rescuer. This enables the rescuer to avoid the direct contact of mouth-to-mouth or mouth-to-nose breathing.

You should keep one tube at home and one in the family car in case of emergency.

SUFFOCATION BY PLASTIC BAG

The widespread use of plastic bags in recent years has created the household hazard of accidental death by suffocation. The great majority of the victims are children under one year of age.

For this reason, one should never leave a plastic bag of any type or size near infants—or in any place within possible reach of children.

Plastic bags have been used by adults in suicide attempts, many proving fatal.

What to Do

1. Remove the bag upon discovery.

2. Immediately begin mouth-to-mouth breathing and continue until the victim breathes for himself.

— 3 —

HOW TO CONTROL HEAVY EXTERNAL BLEEDING

1. If there is a third person on the scene, have him call for medical help immediately.

2. Remove sufficient clothing to see all wounds clearly.

3. Apply a pressure dressing to the wound, using a folded clean handkerchief, part of a clean shirt or sheet, or a clean towel—if you do not have sterile dressings available.

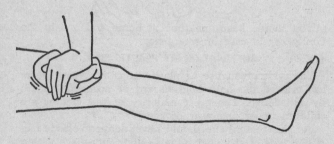

4. Sustain the pressure with your hand for several minutes.

5. If you have no sterile or clean materials, do not hesitate to use clothing or *any* material or even your bare hand in an effort to stop the bleeding. Heavy blood loss is more serious than the danger of infection.

6. If the bleeding is coming from an arm or leg, elevate the limb above the level of the heart and keep it supported with pillows, any kind of thick padding, or furniture. **Do not** move an extremity if you think a bone may be broken.

7. If bleeding continues despite pressure and elevation, press *hard* with your fingers or hand against the artery at the proper pressure point (see illustrations) which restricts the flow of blood to the wounded area.

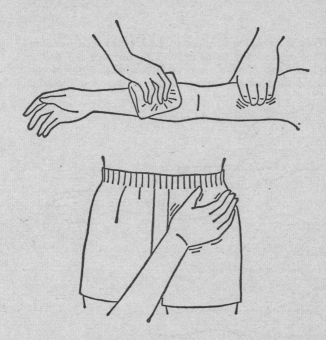

8. Only if heavy bleeding continues despite constant firm pressure over the wound or on the nearby artery should a tourniquet be applied (see illustrations). Since a tourniquet can be dangerous, its use should generally be limited to situations in which there is partial or complete amputation of a body part. There should be unbroken skin between the wound and the tourniquet.

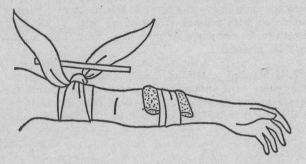

Wrap a strong, wide piece of cloth (such as a handkerchief or necktie) twice around the arm or leg and tie a half knot. Place a short stick (or similar object such as a ruler) on the half knot and . . .

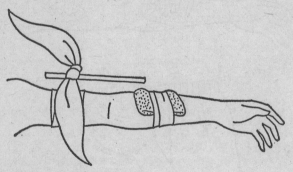

. . . tie a square knot.

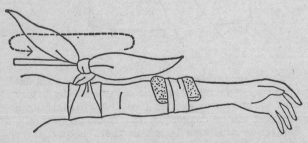

Twist the stick to tighten the tourniquet until the bleeding stops.

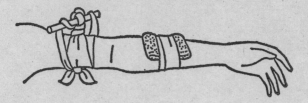

Hold the stick in place with the end of the tourniquet or another strip of cloth.

9. Once the bleeding has stopped, do not attempt to cleanse or otherwise disturb the wound, as you may start it bleeding again.

10. Wrap gauze bandage or cloth firmly around the pressure dressing several times to hold it securely in place.

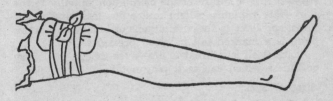

11. If a doctor has not yet arrived on the scene, see that the person gets taken to the nearest hospital.

— 4 —

SHOCK

Shock often accompanies severe injuries, severe infections, extreme pain, hemorrhage, burns, heat exhaustion, food or chemical poisoning, heart attacks, and some strokes. It is a failure of the circulation, initially to the skin (this explains pallor) and other less vital structures, and later to the vital organs of kidney and brain; there is a marked fall in blood pressure.

Shock itself is a threat to life—even though the injury or illness which causes it may not be.

Signs of Shock

1. The face, lips, and fingernails are usually pale.

2. The skin is cold and moist; often there are beads of perspiration on the forehead.

3. The victim often complains of feeling cold and thirsty.

4. He is often nauseated and may vomit.

5. The breathing is shallow and rapid.

6. The pulse, if felt at all, is weak and rapid.

7. The victim may be restless, anxious, semiconscious, or unconscious.

What to Do

1. Keep the victim lying flat on his back. (If he has difficulty in breathing, he may be more comfortable with his head and chest elevated.)

2. If heavy bleeding is the apparent cause of shock, this must be treated first (pp. 30-33).

3. Turn his head to one side so that blood, vomitus, and/or other fluids can flow easily from the mouth, and so that his tongue will stay forward and leave the air passage free.

4. Elevate the victim's legs, keeping the head lower than the trunk of the body—unless he has sustained a head injury or broken bones, or if this position results in pain or difficulty in breathing.

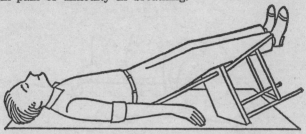

5. Keep the victim warm with blankets or coats, if the weather is cold or damp.

6. Reassure the victim, as fear aggravates shock.

7. Call a physician.

8. If the victim is completely conscious and able to swallow, *and if* he is not nauseated or vomiting, give fluids (water, tea, coffee, broth). If available, prepare a solution using one teaspoon of table salt and one half teaspoon of baking soda (or bicarbonate of soda) to one quart of water.

Whatever fluids you give him, start with a few sips at a time to make sure he will retain it. Gradually increase the amount to approximately one-half a glass (or one cup) every fifteen minutes.

9. Don't give alcohol in any form.

10. Don't give anything by mouth if abdominal injury is suspected.

HOW TO FEEL AND COUNT A PULSE

On certain occasions it is very helpful for the doctor (when he is reached on the telephone) to know the patient's pulse rate. You can learn to feel your own pulse and this will give you experience and confidence in feeling the pulse of someone else.

Every major artery has a pulse, and many arteries travel close enough to the body surface for the pulse to be felt. The easiest place to feel the pulse is at the wrist (see illustration). Hold the wrist so that the balls of your four fingers are over the pulse and your thumb is against the top of the wrist for support. Exert slight pressure with your four fingers until you feel the pulse most strongly.

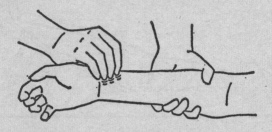

Once you have felt the pulse, you are ready to count it. For this you need a second hand on a clock or watch. Count the number of pulse beats which you feel within any thirty-second period and multiply by two to get the pulse rate (per minute). Repeat this at least once as a check on your accuracy.

Note whether the pulse is strong and easily felt or is weak and difficult to feel—and whether the pulse is regular or irregular. You may be able to determine this by nodding your head with each pulse beat.

— 5 —

CHOKING

(Foreign Body in the Throat or Windpipe)

If the foreign body is causing interference with breathing, there is **no** time to call the physician—unless a third person present does so.

If the victim is having obvious difficulty getting his breath, or if his lips, tongue, or fingernails are bluish in color, **start treatment immediately. Only if there is a third person present should attempts be made to reach a doctor, ambulance, or police.** (The brain can survive undamaged only four minutes without air—speed can mean the difference between life and death in relieving a choking victim.)

What to Do for an Infant

1. Hold the baby by his ankles, letting the head hang straight down.

2. Open the baby's mouth; pull the tongue forward so the obstruction may come out. If it does not, reach into the back of the throat with the index finger and attempt to pull out the obstruction.

3. Hit the baby hard with your hand between the shoulder blades to try to dislodge the object.

4. If you cannot easily remove the obstruction within one minute, begin mouth-to-mouth breathing (pp. 23-26). It is important to get air into the lungs, even if it has to be blown past the obstructing foreign body.

5. Begin mouth-to-mouth breathing (pp. 23-26) if there is no spontaneous breathing after you have removed the object.

What to Do for a Child

1. Hold the child bent head down over your arm or leg.

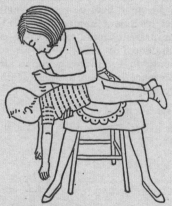

2. Hit the child hard several times with your hand between the shoulder blades.

3. Clear the throat quickly with your index finger and pull the tongue forward.

4. If you cannot easily remove the obstruction within one minute, begin mouth-to-mouth breathing (pp. 23-26). It is important to get air into the lungs, even if it has to be blown past the obstructing foreign body.

5. Begin mouth-to-mouth breathing (pp. 23-26) if there is no spontaneous breathing after you have removed the object.

What to Do for an Adult

1. Have the patient bend forward or lie face down on a bed, sofa, or table with his head and shoulders hanging over the side. If it is impossible to get the victim into one of these positions, roll him on one side or the other, either on the ground or floor.

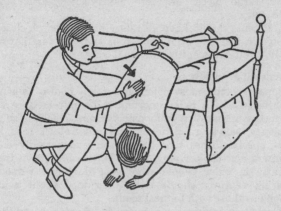

2. Slap his back hard between the shoulder blades.

3. Clear the victim's throat quickly with your index finger and make sure the tongue is pulled forward.

4. If you cannot easily remove the obstruction within one minute, begin mouth-to-mouth breathing (pp. 26-29). It is important to get air into the lungs, even if it has to be blown past the obstructing foreign body.

5. If there is no spontaneous breathing after you have removed the object, begin mouth-to-mouth breathing (pp. 26-29).

Prevention in Children

The National Safety Council lists choking on foreign bodies as the leading cause of accidental deaths in the home in children under six years of age. Good preventive measures include:

1. Parents should not hold such objects as pins and tacks in their mouths because children quickly imitate the practice.

2. Children under four years old should not be allowed to eat nuts, raw fruit, or raw vegetables. These foods require the grinding of the molars. Since the first set of teeth do not come through completely until the child is two years old or more and the chewing habit is not firmly established until the age of four years, large pieces of these foods can obstruct the child's airway.

3. Parents should keep all safety pins closed. A closed safety pin usually is not dangerous and will pass harmlessly through the entire intestinal tract.

Prevention in Adults

Bones are the most common foreign bodies causing choking in adults. It is important to be extremely careful in the preparation of foods containing chicken (such as soups, salads, sandwiches, and casseroles). It is in these special dishes that the person unexpectedly encounters and chokes on a bone. This occurs more frequently in older people who wear dentures. Persons wearing dentures should chew their food about twice as long as those with natural teeth.

Alcohol is frequently a factor in choking in adults. Due to the dulling effect of alcohol upon concentration and co-ordination, the person under its influence is more apt to choke on food.

— 6 —

MOVING AN INJURED PERSON

An injured person should never be moved by an untrained rescuer, except to prevent further injury and
possible death—for example, in case of fire, smoke,
flood, or explosion. Improper transportation can do
irreparable harm.

It usually takes two or three people to carry an
adult. This chapter is written for the lone, untrained
rescuer who **must** remove someone, whether injured or
not, from a perilous situation.

Aiding a Victim Who Can Walk

1. Help the victim to stand, making certain that both
your footing and his are sound.

2. Stand to one side of him, facing in the same direction.

3. Pass his arm nearest you up around the back of your neck and down onto your chest, holding his hand with your corresponding hand.

4. Your other arm should support the victim around his waist.

5. If the victim gets too tired, it is very easy to switch to the pack-strap carry (pp. 45-46).

**Carrying a Victim Who Is Conscious
but Cannot Walk**

If the victim is not too heavy, use the **arms carry:**

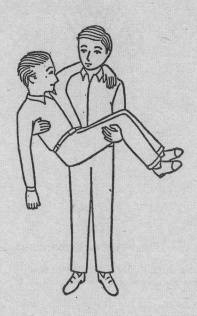

1. Place him on his back.

2. Kneel on one knee.

3. Slide your arm under his knees.

4. Place your other arm under his back at the level of his shoulder blades, reaching under the far armpit.

5. Raise him to your knee.

6. Roll him against your chest.

7. Then stand and walk.

If the victim is too heavy to be picked up and carried in your arms, use the **piggy-back carry:**

1. Place the person face down on his stomach.

2. Straddle him, facing his head, and lift him up to his knees by the armpits.

3. After he is on his knees, slide your arms down around his chest and raise him to his feet.

4. Move quickly in front of him so your back supports his weight.

5. Bend far forward and hunch him high onto your back.

6. Slide your arms around and underneath the victim's thighs.

7. Have him clasp his hands across your chest.

8. If he cannot do so, grasp his right wrist with your left hand and his left wrist with your right hand.

9. Then walk.

Carrying a Victim Who Is Unconscious or Cannot Help

If the victim is too heavy to be picked up and carried in your arms, use the **pack-strap carry**:

1. Lie down parallel to the victim with your back against his chest.

2. In this position reach over him and bring his top arm over your shoulder. Hold it in place with your hand close to your chest.

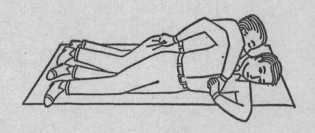

3. With your other hand grasp the victim's clothing at his hip.

4. Then roll him over on top of you.

5. From this position get onto your knees.

6. Get up on one knee and then stand upright.

7. Now you are in a position to walk.

Or

If the victim is too heavy to be picked up and carried in your arms, you may use the **fireman's carry:**

1. Place the victim face down on his stomach.

2. Kneel on one knee at the victim's head, facing him.

3. Place one hand under each shoulder, and begin to lift him.

4. Slide each hand further down the side of his chest and across his back.

5. Raise him to his knees and then to his feet.

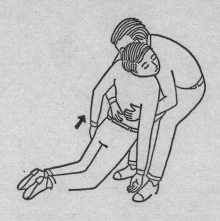

6. Place your left leg between the victim's legs.

7. Grab his right wrist with your left hand, duck under his right arm with your head, and lift his arm around the back of your neck.

8. With your right hand, clasp his right lower thigh.

9. Balancing the victim across your shoulders, straighten up and walk.

10. If you later wish to free your left hand, you may transfer the victim's right hand to your right hand.

Part Two

ACCIDENTS

— 7 —

POISONING AND OVERDOSAGE

OF MEDICINE

Every year in the United States approximately fifteen hundred people die from accidental poisoning. *Non*-fatal accidents of this kind number a staggering five hundred thousand annually. Of these, about half are caused by medications and half by household products, and 90 per cent of the victims are children under five years of age.

The most common poison is aspirin—causing one hundred thousand childhood poisonings yearly, and 144 deaths in 1964. The next most common causes are: insecticides (frequently due to parents' storing of insect-killer concentrates in soda pop bottles), bleach, detergents, soaps and cleaners, furniture polish, kerosene, vitamins and iron, disinfectants (such as iodine) and deodorizers, lye and corrosives, and laxatives.

Of the more than two hundred and fifty thousand potentially poisonous household products which can be bought in your neighborhood stores, a large percentage are not labeled "poison." Many of these substances might be tolerated by an adult, but would be poisonous to children. Anything can be poisonous if taken in large enough doses, depending on what the substance is, how much is taken, and the size and age of the individual.

Prevention

Almost all accidents of this kind *can* be prevented— if you make the following safety rules a permanent part of your everyday life:

1. Keep all medicines out of the reach of children— store them in locked cabinets or closets, if possible.

2. Always refer to medicine by its proper name— never tell a child that medicine is candy.

3. Never, even for a moment, leave discarded medi-

51

cines where children might get at them—such as on night stands, living room table tops, and in the bathroom. Young children love to explore pocketbooks, so if you carry pills in your pocketbook be careful where you leave it.

4. Do not use the contents of an unlabeled bottle— even if you think you remember what it contains.

5. Never take or give any medication without **reading the label twice**—this means no taking or giving medicines in the dark.

6. If there is any question about the dosage of medicine, check with your doctor or druggist before using it.

7. Put your medicines away immediately after using them.

8. Clean out your medicine cabinets regularly; discard prescriptions no longer needed. As a general rule, most medicines should not be kept for more than one year, as their effectiveness may be altered.

9. Discarded liquid medicines should be flushed down the toilet, and solid preparations should be burned or incinerated immediately.

10. Use prescription medicines only for the person for whom they were ordered.

11. All medicines and household products should remain in their labeled containers, and these containers should be rinsed immediately when they are empty, then discarded right away.

12. If you transfer drugs, pills, or poisonous substances, label the new containers.

13. Household preparations such as detergents, cleaning and polishing agents, lye, insecticides, and kerosene should be stored in cabinets high above the reach of children.

14. Hazardous products should always be returned to a safe storage place **immediately** after use and not left around the house on furniture, window sills, floors, in the basement, on the back porch, or in the garage.

15. Nonedible products should never be kept in food storage areas or in beverage or food containers.

16. Be sure to protect your skin when using solvents, strong cleaning agents, and insecticides, as some chemicals can be absorbed through the skin. Should you get an insecticide on your skin, wash it off immediately with soap and water.

17. Never use insecticide sprays in front of children.

18. Follow the directions on the container for the safe use of every product.

19. Be especially careful **a)** when you are moving or going on vacation, as medicines and other poisonous substances are apt to be out of their normal places—and **b)** when you are sick, menstruating, pregnant, emotionally upset, or preoccupied.

20. Call your doctor immediately if someone in your home has swallowed a potentially poisonous substance —do not wait for symptoms to appear.

21. Instruct any household help or baby-sitters in the basic rules of safety listed above.

When to Suspect Poisoning

Whenever children have been left unattended and there is possible access to any poisonous material, look for discoloration of the lips and mouth resulting from paint, powder, or other colored material, wild berries, or leaves.

Smell the breath to detect any unusual odor. Look for any bottles or packages of drugs or other poisonous material that have been left open.

Be suspicious if the person **1)** complains of burning in the mouth or throat; **2)** behaves peculiarly or is confused; or **3)** is excessively drowsy or difficult to arouse.

SWALLOWED POISONS

Household Chemicals

Call your doctor or nearest Poison Control Center **immediately**—even if you are not positive that the substance swallowed is poisonous. They can tell you whether it is poisonous and give you specific instructions.

Speed is essential. If possible, one person should begin treatment while another is telephoning. Save any suspected poison and its container (if possible, use the antidote recommended on the label)—and any material which is vomited, as this may give an invaluable clue to the type of poison. If the nature of the poison is unknown, give one teaspoonful ipecac syrup or activated charcoal mixed with water as a first-aid measure. If you do not have either on hand, give milk or water—one to two cups from ages one to five, and up to one quart if five years of age or over.

Do not make the person vomit IF:

1. He has swallowed any material listed on the next page (many household substances contain **lye**, which may rupture the esophagus if vomited, and petroleum products such as **kerosene**, which may pass into the lungs and damage them in the course of vomiting).

2. He is already vomiting or complaining of severe pains in the mouth or throat.

3. He is unconscious or is in convulsions.

DO NOT INDUCE VOMITING...

...if the person has swallowed anything listed below. Give milk or water—one to two cups from ages one to five, and up to one quart if five years of age or over.

▲ AMMONIA
  BENZINE
▲ BLEACH (HOUSEHOLD)
  CARBOLIC ACID
    DISINFECTANTS
  CORN AND WART
    REMOVERS
  CREOSOTE
▲ DETERGENTS
▲ DRAIN CLEANERS
  DRY CLEANING FLUIDS
  FLOOR WAX AND POLISHES
  FURNITURE WAX AND
    POLISHES
  GASOLINE
  GREASE REMOVERS
  GUN CLEANERS
▲ HAIR STRAIGHTENERS
  INK ERADICATORS
  KEROSENE
  LIGHTER FLUID
▲ LIME

▲ LYE
  LYSOL
  METAL CLEANERS
  NAPHTHA
  OVEN CLEANERS
  PAINT BRUSH CLEANERS
  PAINT THINNERS AND
    REMOVERS
  PINE OIL
  PLASTIC CEMENT
  RUBBER CEMENT
  RUST REMOVERS
▲ SODIUM CARBONATE
  STRONG ACIDS
  STRYCHNINE RAT POISONS
  TOILET BOWL CLEANERS
  TURPENTINE
  TYPEWRITER CLEANERS
  VARNISH REMOVERS
▲ WASHING SODA
  WOOD PRESERVATIVES

▲ Vinegar or any fruit juice may be given as well as milk or water, for these poisons are alkali-corrosives.

If the person has swallowed anything listed on the following page, **give milk or water**—one to two cups from ages one to five, and up to one quart if five years of age or over. **Then**

INDUCE VOMITING ...

... by 1) placing your finger or the handle of a spoon at the back of the throat; or 2) giving two tablespoons of ordinary table salt in a glass of warm water; or 3) giving warm soap solution.

When retching and vomiting begin, place the victim lying face down, with his head lower than his hips (this prevents vomitus from entering the lungs and causing further damage).

HOUSEHOLD ITEMS

AFTER SHAVE LOTIONS

ALCOHOL (RUBBING, ETHYL)

ALCOHOL (WOOD, METHYL)

ANT AND MOUSE BAITS

ANTIFREEZE

ANTISEPTIC DETERGENTS

ARSENIC RAT POISON

BORAX

CAMPHOR AND MOTH
   REPELLENTS

CANNED HEAT

CRAYONS (especially red or
   orange)

DDT INSECT POISONS

DEODORANTS

DRY SHAMPOOS

FIREWORKS

FLEA POWDER

FORMALDEHYDE

FRECKLE REMOVER

HAIR DYES

INK (blue or black ink is
   not poisonous)

LINIMENTS

LIQUOR OR BEER (in children)

MATCHES

NAIL POLISH

NAIL POLISH REMOVERS
   (ACETONE)

PAINTS

PERFUME

PERMANENT WAVE SOLUTION
   (NEUTRALIZERS)

SHELLAC

SHOE POLISHES

SILVER POLISH

SUN TAN PREPARATIONS

VARNISHES

MEDICINES

ARTHRITIS REMEDIES

ASPIRIN AND OTHER PAIN
   RELIEVERS

BARBITURATES

▲ BORIC ACID

CORTISONE

COUGH REMEDIES

DIGITALIS AND OTHER
   HEART MEDICINES

DOUCHE PREPARATIONS

EYE DROPS (ATROPINE)

IODINE—Induce vomiting
   by giving 1 heaping
   tablespoon of corn-
   starch or flour per
   pint of water

IRON PILLS AND SYRUP

LAXATIVES

PAREGORIC

"PEP" DRUGS

REDUCING MEDICINES

SLEEPING DRUGS

TRANQUILIZERS

VITAMINS

▲ Boric acid should not be kept in the house. It is not

the treatment of choice for diaper rash or any other common ailment. Poisoning can occur when boric acid is mistaken for a baby's formula mix, or when it is used to treat diaper rash or a cut on the skin.

LEAD

Lead can be a fatal poison—or it can result in paralysis, permanent brain damage, or mental retardation.

Lead poisoning occurs most often in children (aged one and a half to three years) who eat small pieces of dried lead paint from the walls or peelings which drop from ceilings, especially in older buildings. Or children may chew on window sills, water and gas pipes, fire escapes, plaster, or window putty.

Lead poisoning is most commonly due to the gradual but steady accumulation of lead in the system. Any of the following may be symptoms or signs of lead poisoning:

> Poor appetite
> Stomach ache
> Repeated vomiting
> Constipation
> Headaches
> Paleness
> Crankiness
> Convulsions
> Coma

If any of your children has one or more of these signs, inform your doctor immediately. The earlier lead poisoning is found and treated, the better the chances are for complete recovery.

Acute poisoning by the swallowing of lead is rare and results frequently in vomiting and abdominal pains. If poisoning is due to the intake of a single dose, **induce vomiting** by 1) placing your finger or the handle of a spoon at the back of the throat; or 2) giving two tablespoons of ordinary table salt in a glass of warm water; or 3) giving warm soap solution. **After vomiting, or if vomiting is not immediately induced, give the victim two or three glasses of milk.**

The inhalation of lead from the burning of lead storage battery casings may result in mild to profound poisoning, with mental and behavioral changes, including delirium and convulsions. Upon any suspicion, **remove the person to uncontaminated air.** If excitement or convulsions occur, then **1)** protect the patient from harm to himself; **2)** reduce light and noise to a minimum; **3)** call the doctor; and **4)** keep the person quiet and comfortably warm without unnecessary movement until the doctor comes.

Prevention

In recent years most indoor paint has been made safe. However, most outdoor paint contains large amounts of lead. So *do not use any outdoor paint to paint anything inside your house or apartment.*

If you do not understand the label on a can of paint you are planning to use, take it to your paint store and ask if the paint contains lead (less than 1 per cent is allowable). If you are not certain your paint is safe, do not use it. *Buy only paint you can be sure is safe.*

The labeling of children's furniture and toys and play materials has severely curtailed the use of lead paint, but another hazard has recently been discovered —the use of *lead compounds in the manufacture of beads such as "fake" pearls and household articles of plastic material with a pearly luster.* Never give anything of this nature as a plaything to young children.

Although not related to lead, there is another poison hazard in the form of beads in necklaces, rosaries, or decorations made from the *jequirity bean,* which comes from the Caribbean, Mexico, or South America. In its natural state it is a small scarlet bean with a black spot and its inner meat is very poisonous, especially when chewed. If swallowed whole, poisoning is unlikely as the hard seed coat prevents rapid absorption. Check your jewelry, and if you have any jequirity beans in the house, see that young children have no possible access to them.

Overdosage of Medicines and Drugs

One of the difficulties in the recognition of poisoning by medicinal overdosage is that immediate symptoms may be entirely absent. The suspicion of poisoning may be first aroused by the finding of an opened medicine container or noticing missing tablets.

When overdosage is suspected, call the doctor immediately. He will want to know 1) **what the medicine is**; 2) **how much was swallowed**; 3) **how much time has elapsed since the intake.** His advice will depend upon this information.

Meanwhile, it is essential to **act without delay** (before symptoms develop) to dilute and then remove the swallowed poison. **Give the person milk or water—** one to two cups from ages one to five, and up to one quart if five years of age or over.

Then **induce vomiting** by 1) placing your finger or the handle of a spoon at the back of the throat; or 2) giving two tablespoons of ordinary table salt in a glass of warm water; or 3) giving warm soap solution.

Never induce vomiting if the patient is unconscious or having convulsions. **Do not give any alcoholic beverages.**

FOOD POISONING

Despite great strides which have been made in the preparation, preservation, and inspection of fresh, canned and frozen foods and beverages, food poisoning is still a major hazard to health and sometimes to life itself.

The *symptoms of food poisoning* can vary from mild abdominal discomfort and diarrhea to severe nausea, vomiting, abdominal pains, watery or bloody diarrhea, chills, fever, extreme general weakness, and even various muscle weaknesses and paralyses.

What to Do

Call your doctor immediately. If you cannot reach him right away and there is the suspicion of having eaten contaminated food within the past four hours, **induce vomiting if vomiting has not already begun** by 1) placing your finger or the handle of a spoon at the back of the throat; or 2) giving two tablespoons of ordinary table salt in a glass of warm water; or 3) giving warm soap solution.

Save any possibly contaminated food for later examination.

Prevention

Keep all cooking and serving utensils clean. Make sure your hands are thoroughly washed before the handling and preparation of any food.

Canned foods which are processed at home should be prepared according to definite government standards. Pamphlets are obtainable from the Superintendent of Documents, Government Printing Office, Washington, D.C. 20025.

The following foods should never be allowed to remain at room temperature for more than an hour: fish, meat, milk, cream, whipped cream, cheese, mayonnaise, eggs, ice cream, custards and puddings, cream-filled bakery goods. *Do not eat or serve anything which smells or looks unusual.* Frozen foods should never be refrozen once thawed.

Boiling, broiling, frying, or pressure cooking for at least fifteen minutes will reduce to a minimum the possibilities of bacterial or toxic contamination.

Sodium nitrite, which is used to preserve the color of meat in pickling or salting processes, should never be used or kept in the home.

Mushrooms and Other Poisonous Plants

Poisonous mushrooms may grow where non-poisonous mushrooms grow. Over a hundred fatalities occur each year in the United States alone from eating poisonous mushrooms. Swallowing even part of one mushroom of a deadly species can be fatal. For these reasons, *one should never pick or eat wild mushrooms.*

Symptoms: Different types of poisonous mushrooms cause different symptoms. Some occur within a matter of minutes, while others may occur only after an interval of six to twenty-four hours. Symptoms may vary from severe nausea, vomiting, and diarrhea to salivation, wheezing, muscular shaking and profound mental excitement, confusion, and delirium.

What to Do

Call a physician or get to a hospital as quickly as possible. Until medical assistance is available, **induce vomiting** by 1) placing your finger or the handle of a spoon at the back of the throat; or 2) giving two tablespoons of ordinary table salt in a glass of warm water; or 3) giving warm soap solution.

Other Poisonous Plants

It is not within the scope of this book to describe in

detail the enormous number of plant hazards to which humans are exposed. Some plants may be mildly toxic, while others can be fatal, even if only a part of the plant is swallowed. Therefore, *never eat wild plants* unless you are absolutely certain of their identity. In addition, never allow children to chew on or eat any indoor plants.

The following list comprises the most common offenders:

POISONOUS PLANTS

Name	Part of Plant
Akee (Blighia sapida)	Unopened, unripe fruit, seeds
Arnica (Arnica montana)	Flowers
Arum family: calla lily, elephant-ear Dieffenbachia, Caladium, Alocasia, Colocasia, Philodendron), Dracunculus, Amorphophallis	All parts
Beechnut (Fagus sylvatica)	Seeds
Betelnut (Areca catechu)	Seeds
Bird of Paradise (Caesalpinia gilliesii)	Seeds and pods
Bittersweet (Solanum dulcamarum)	Leaves and fruit
Black henbane (Hyoscyamus niger)	All parts
Black nightshade (Solanum nigrum)	Leaves and green fruit
Bloodroot (Sanguinaria canadensis)	All parts and especially rootstalk
Box (Buxus sempervirens)	Leaves and twigs
Buckeye bush (Euonymus atropurpureus)	Fruit and leaves
Calabar bean (Physostigma venenosum)	Bean
Cashew nut (Anacardium occidentale)	Oil
Cassava (Manihot utilissima)	Root

Name	*Part of Plant*
Castor bean (Ricinus communis)	Seed
Celandine (Chelidonium majus)	All parts and especially root
Cherry, black (Prunus serotina)	Bark, leaves, but especially the seed
Cockles (Agrostemma githago)	Seeds

Colchicum
  Meadow saffron
  Autumn crocus
  Naked-ladies
    (Colchicum autumnale)
	Seeds, leaves, flowers

Croton (Croton tiglium)	Seed (croton oil)
Crowfoot family:	All parts
Christmas rose (Helleborus niger)	All parts
Crowfoot or buttercup (Ranunculaceae)	All parts
Golden seal (Hydrastis canadensis)	All parts
Larkspur (Delphinium)	All parts
Marsh marigold (Caltha palustris)	All parts
Monkshood (Aconitum columbianum)	All parts, but especially roots and seed
Daffodil-Jonquil (Narcissus pseudonarcissus)	Bulb
Daphne	All parts
Darnel (Lolium temulentum)	Seed
Deadly nightshade (Atropa belladonna)	Berries, leaves, and roots
Death camas (Zygadenus)	Bulb or root
Elderberry, black elder (Sambucus canadensis)	Leaves, shoots, and bark
False hellebore (Veratrum viride)	All parts

Fava bean (Vicia fava)
  Broad bean
  Horse bean
  Windsor bean
	Pollen and bean

Name	Part of Plant
Finger cherry (Rhodomyrtus macrocarpa	Fruit
Fish berries (Cocculus indicus)	Dried fruit
Foxglove (Digitalis purpurea, D. lanata)	Leaves
Gloriosa or climbing lily	All parts, especially the tuber
Henbane, black (Hyoscyamus niger)	All parts
Holly, black alder (Ilex aquifolium, opaca, etc.)	Berries
Hydrangea, wild hydrangea	Under normal conditions this plant is non-toxic. However, formation of hydrocyanic acid is possible and may cause symptoms.
Indian tobacco (Lobelia inflata)	All parts
Iris (Iridaceae)	Root
Jequirity bean (Abrus precatorius) Love bean Rosary bean Lucky bean Prayer bean	Bean (if thoroughly chewed. If swallowed whole, poisoning is unlikely since hard seed coat prevents rapid absorption.)
Jerusalem cherry (Solanum pseudocapsicum)	Fruit
Jessamine or yellow jessamine (Gelsemium sempervirens)	All parts
Jet berry bush (Rhodotypos) (An ornamental bush with black berries)	All parts
Jimson weed or thorn apple, stinkweed, etc. (Datura stramonium)	All parts

Name	*Part of Plant*
Jute (Corchorus olitorius, C. capsulatus)	Fibrous stem
Kentucky coffee tree (Gymnoclaudus dioica)	Seed
Laburnum (Cytisus laburnum)	Leaves and seeds
Lady's slipper (Cypripedium hirsutum)	Hairs of stems and leaves
Lantana (L. camara)	All parts
Laurel (mountain, black, sheep, American, etc.) (Kalmia)	All parts
Lily of the valley (Convallaria majalis)	Leaves and flowers
Locust, black (Robinia pseudoacacia)	Seed
Lupin (Lupinus sp.)	All parts, but especially the berries
Manchineel (Hippomane mancinela)	Sap
Mango (Mangifera indica)	Skin (peel) of fruit and sap of tree
Marijuana (Cannabis sativa)	Leaves
Mescal, peyote (Lophophora williamsii)	Button (Mescaline)
Mistletoe (Phoradendron flavescens)	All parts, but especially the berries
Mushrooms (Amanita, Muscaria, and Phalloides)	See p. 59.
Oleander (Nerium oleander)	Leaves
Peas (Lathyrus sp.)	Seeds
Physic nut (Jatropha sp.)	Seed
Poison ivy, poison oak, poison creeper, picry, mercury (Rhus toxicondendron)	All parts can cause skin lesions (see pp. 188–201)
Poison sumac, poison dogwood, poison elder, poison ash, swamp sumac, thunderwood (Rhus vernix)	All parts can cause skin lesions (see pp. 188–201)

Name	*Part of Plant*
Poison hemlock, deadly hemlock, poison parsley (Conium maculatum)	All parts
Poinsettia (Euphorbia pulcherrima)	Leaves, stem, and milky sap
Pokewood, poke berry, scoke, ink berry (Phytolacca americana)	All parts, but especially root
Poppy (Papaver somniferum)	Unripe seed capsule
Potato (Solanum tuberosum)	Green tubers, new sprouts
Primrose (Primula sp.)	Stems and leaves
Privet, common (Ligustrum vulgare)	Leaves and berries
Pyracantha, fire-thorn (Pyracantha coccinea)	Shrub bearing clusters of small bright red and orange berrylike fruit
Rayless goldenrod (Haplopappus heterophyllus)	All parts
Rhododendron	All parts
Rhubarb-pie plant (Rheum sp.)	Leaves
Snakeroot, white (Eupatorium urticae folium)	All parts
Spanish broom (Sparteus junceum, Sarothamnus scoparius)	Seeds or leaves
Spindle tree (Euonymus europaea)	Fruit and leaves
Stagger bush (Lyonia)	All parts
Star anise (Japanese)	All parts
Tung nut (Aleurites fordii)	Seed
Water hemlock Cowbane Beaver poison (Cicuta maculata and Conium)	Roots

Name	Part of Plant
Wild aconite (Monkshood) (Aconitum and other species)	All parts
Wild grape (Rhiocissus cuneifolia)	Root
Wild tomato Horse nettle Bull nettle Sand briar (Solanum carolinense)	Green fruit
Wisteria (W. chinensis)	Pods
Yellow nightshade (Urechites suberecta)	Fruit
Yew (Taxus)	All parts

Poisonous Fish

Certain shellfish, marine and fresh-water fish may be poisonous when eaten, even though properly prepared, stored, and cooked. This is true because they contain toxins which survive cooking and are due to 1) the chemistry of the fish itself; or 2) poisonous organisms in the water which are taken in by the fish as food.

The most common offenders in this type of poisoning are: some mussels, rarely clams and oysters, globefish (also called puffers or blowfish), some forms of triggerfish, parrotfish, wrasse, porcupine fish, moray eels, barracuda, and surmullet (also called goatfish).

The **symptoms of acute seafood poisoning** may appear within ten minutes after eating or may be delayed for many hours. They vary from nausea, vomiting and diarrhea to numbness and tingling, muscular weakness, staggering, paralysis, or mental symptoms.

What to Do

Call a physician or get to a hospital as quickly as possible. Until medical assistance is available, **induce vomiting** by 1) placing your finger or the handle of a spoon at the back of the throat; or 2) giving two tablespoons of ordinary table salt in a glass of warm water; or 3) giving warm soap solution.

INHALED POISONS

This is probably the most insidious form of all types of accidental poisoning, as the victim does not realize he is in danger. It is essential to know the types of substances which can cause inhalation poisoning, to use them only in well-ventilated rooms, and to avoid prolonged breathing of their vapors.

Among the commonest causes of inhalation poisoning are:

ALCOHOL (WOOD, METHYL)
AMMONIA
ANTIFREEZE
BENZENE
CARBON MONOXIDE
CARBON TETRACHLORIDE AND OTHER DRY CLEANING FLUIDS
DEMOTHING AGENTS (NAPHTHALENE)
FIRE EXTINGUISHING FLUIDS
FLEA POWDER
FORMALDEHYDE
FUMIGANTS (CYANIDE)
NAIL POLISH REMOVERS (ACETONE)
PAINT REMOVERS
PAINTS
RAT POISONS (PHOSPHORUS, ARSENIC)
SHELLACS
STOVE AND SHOE POLISHES
TURPENTINE
VARNISHES

Warning: Bleaches and powerful household cleansers, such as those used for ovens and toilet bowls, should *not* be mixed with each other—or with household ammonia or vinegar. Such combinations may release chlorine gas or other irritating and harmful gases.

What to Do

1. Carry or drag the victim—do not let him walk—to fresh air immediately.

2. Open all doors and windows.

3. Loosen all tight clothing.

4. Begin mouth-to-mouth breathing (pp. 23-29) if his breathing has stopped or is irregular.

5. Call your doctor.

6. In the meantime, keep the person warm by wrapping him in blankets and keep him as quiet as possible.

7. If he is having convulsions, keep him in bed in a semidark room and avoid jarring or noise.

8. **Do not give alcohol in any form.**

9. Do not become a victim yourself by exposure to the same poison.

SKIN CONTAMINATION BY CHEMICALS

Many of the same chemicals which are poisonous when swallowed or inhaled are also toxic when they come into contact with the skin. The severity of the poisoning depends upon the nature of the substance and the area of skin surface exposed.

The principal chemical agents which are toxic when absorbed through the skin are:

AMMONIA
ALCOHOL (WOOD, METHYL)
CARBON TETRACHLORIDE AND OTHER DRY CLEANING FLUIDS
DDT AND OTHER INSECTICIDES
FORMALDEHYDE
HAIR DYES
INKS
PAINT REMOVERS
PAINTS
STOVE AND SHOE POLISHES
VARNISHES

What to Do

Drench the skin with water (shower, hose, faucet). Apply the stream of water on the skin while, at the same time, removing clothing. Cleanse the skin thoroughly with water. **Speed** is most important in reducing the extent of the injury.

— 8 —

WOUNDS, CUTS, AND BRUISES

DEEP CUTS

Because these are inflicted by sharp objects such as knives, razors, or broken glass, the edges of this type of wound are usually smooth, not jagged. Infection is infrequent, as little dirt or foreign material gets into a wound of this kind. Bleeding may be profuse and there may be damage to such important structures as arteries, nerves, and tendons.

What to Do

1. Stop heavy bleeding (pp. 30-33).

2. Then call your doctor.

MINOR CUTS

Wash the cut with soap and water, and then cover it with a sterile gauze pad or an adhesive strip bandage.

Call your doctor if pain, redness, swelling, or tenderness increases in the area of the cut—or if it has been contaminated with manure or excrement.

JAGGED CUTS

Jagged cuts, also called lacerations, are caused by blunt instruments or falls against sharp objects. Bleeding is seldom severe. However, important structures such as nerves and tendons may be damaged. The danger of infection is greater in a cut of this kind than in a clean deep cut, and healing is usually slower.

What to Do

1. Wash the cut with soap and water.

2. Cover it with a sterile gauze pad or adhesive strip bandage.

3. Call your doctor.

PUNCTURE OR PENETRATING WOUNDS

These are caused by penetrating objects such as gunshots, nails, fishhooks, knives, and ice picks. The point of entry may be small, but deeper structures including arteries and nerves may be damaged— also such organs as intestine, lung, kidney, spleen, or heart.

Wounds of this type may look harmless on the surface, producing very little *external* bleeding, but can cause serious deep injury and serious infections.

What to Do

1. Call your doctor right away, as all puncture or penetrating wounds should be examined and treated professionally.

2. Keep the victim lying down and quiet.

3. Watch for and treat developing shock (pp. 34-35).

Gunshot Wounds

Gunshot wounds should be treated in the same way as any other puncture or penetrating wound, as previously outlined. However, the course of a missile or bullet, once it has entered the body, may be unpredictable. Always suspect broken bones, internal hemorrhage, and injury to vital organs. If an extremity has been shot, splint it (pp. 77-79) if you have to move the victim.

All instances of gunshot injuries should be reported to the police.

Fishhook Wounds

If a fishhook becomes embedded in the skin and medical aid is not available, do the following—**unless** it has penetrated the face or the skin around the eyes.

1. Press down on the shank of the hook until you have pushed the barbed end all the way through the skin.

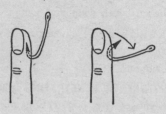

2. Cut off the barbed end with pliers or clippers.

3. Then remove the shaft of the hook.

4. Try to get the wound to bleed.

5. Wash the wound with soap and water.

6. Cover it with a sterile gauze dressing or an adhesive strip bandage.

7. See a physician as soon as possible, as he may want to give you a preventive injection against tetanus.

OPEN ABDOMINAL WOUNDS

These are wounds from which intestines and possibly other organs may protrude.

What to Do

1. Call a doctor **immediately.**
2. Do not give the victim anything by mouth.
3. Do not attempt to replace any protruding abdominal organs.
4. If intestines are exposed, cover them immediately with a sterile dressing or clean cloth, which **must be kept moist.** Add one teaspoon of salt to one pint of water and boil for five minutes. Cool to bath temperature before using to moisten dressing. If this is not possible, keep the dressing moistened with the cleanest water available.
5. Keep the patient warm and lying flat on his back, with his knees bent.
6. Make sure the dressing remains moist until the doctor arrives.

DEEP CHEST WOUNDS

When an object such as a knife, ice pick, or bullet has penetrated through the chest wall, air can be heard passing in and out of the wound, sometimes producing a sucking sound.

This is a serious threat to life, because without first aid it will lead rapidly to total collapse of the lung.

What to Do

1. Place a thick pad of sterile gauze or clean cloth over the wound **at the end of an exhalation** (before the next breath in).
2. Hold the pad in place with firm manual pressure.

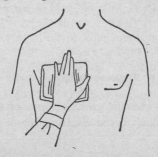

3. Secure the pad firmly with adhesive tape or a belt drawn snugly around the chest. The **important thing is to make sure that no air is leaking through the wound and that you have made an airtight seal.**

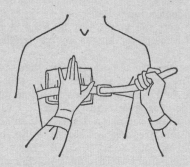

4. Call your doctor, for this injury will require further medical attention and probably hospitalization.

ABRASIONS

These are caused by rubbing or scraping of the skin as when one "skins" his elbow or knee or sustains other scuffing or friction injuries. Only the outer layers of the skin are damaged in an abrasion; a small amount of bleeding may occur, but presents no problem. While dirt and other foreign material may be ground into the abraded skin, there is only slight danger of infection resulting.

What to Do

1. Wash the area gently with soap and water, using sterile or clean gauze or cotton.

2. If available, apply household (3 per cent) hydrogen peroxide with sterile or clean gauze or cotton.

3. Apply petroleum jelly to the area and cover with a sterile gauze dressing. Secure the dressing with adhesive tape. If you do not have sterile or clean gauze available, cover the abrasion with a freshly ironed handkerchief.

4. Keep the abraded area and dressing dry and clean.

5. Do not disturb the dressing for at least twenty-four hours.

6. In removing the dressing, you can minimize any sticking of the scab to the bandage by pouring a small amount of household (3 per cent) hydrogen peroxide onto the bandaged area as you gradually pull the dressing away.

7. Call your doctor if pain, redness, swelling, or tenderness increases in the area of the abrasion—or if dirt or other foreign material is ground into the abrasion.

BRUISES

A bruise, or contusion, is a closed wound caused by the impact of a blunt object or a fall. While the skin is not broken, there is tissue damage underneath and a varying amount of bleeding into the tissues. This produces "black and blue" discoloration if it occurs near enough to the skin surface. If the bleeding occurs deeper in the tissues, there will be no immediate discoloration, but there may be pain and swelling.

What to Do

1. Apply an ice bag, ice pack, or cold compresses immediately to minimize tissue bleeding. Maintain this cold treatment for a period of up to twenty-four hours.

2. Keep the injured area motionless and, if possible, elevate it above the level of the heart for twenty-four hours.

3. After twenty-four hours discontinue the cold treatment and start the application of heat, using hot moist towels which have been wrung out. These may be kept warm by a hot water bottle or an electric heating pad placed on top of them.

Important—Some heating pads are designed to be used safely next to wet surfaces, while others must be protected from the wet towels by plastic or rubber sheeting or oilcloth. This will prevent water from causing a short circuit in the heating pad, which can lead to an electric shock.

Be certain you know which kind of heating pad you have, and act accordingly.

4. Any bruise which after the first twenty-four hours becomes more painful or swollen should be reported to your doctor.

SPLINTERS

If the splinter is near the surface of the skin, you can easily remove it by following the steps below. (If it is deeply imbedded, have your doctor remove it.)

What to Do

1. Sterilize a needle and tweezers by holding the tips in a flame for a few seconds.

2. Press firmly against the skin near the point of the splinter, stroking it toward the point of entry.

3. Grasp the loosened end of the splinter with tweezers and pull it out at the same angle that it entered the skin.

4. Try to make the wound bleed.

5. Wash the wound with soap and water.

6. Cover it with a sterile gauze dressing or an adhesive strip bandage.

— 9 —

BROKEN BONES

NECK OR SPINE INJURIES

Proper emergency care in these injuries can mean the difference between life and death—between complete recovery and permanent paralysis. This is especially true in neck injuries.

Whenever a person has a pain in the back or neck following an accident, consider the possibility of a spinal injury and act accordingly.

So-called "whiplash" injuries to the neck are extremely common in automobile accidents. The pain and stiffness which they produce usually come on hours after the accident and get worse before they begin to improve. It is important for a doctor to examine a person with a suspected "whiplash" injury so that he can make an accurate diagnosis and prescribe accordingly.

What to Do

1. Do not move the victim or lift his head—even to shift him into a more comfortable position—until he has been examined by a physician.

2. Keep the victim comfortably warm and absolutely quiet until medical help arrives.

3. Watch the victim's breathing. Be prepared to use mouth-to-mouth breathing (pp. 23-29) if necessary.

4. Do not move his head.

FRACTURES OF THE ARMS, LEGS, HANDS, AND FEET

The aim of first-aid treatment of broken bones is to minimize pain and prevent further injury. Fractures can be closed (simple) or open (compound), depending on whether the skin is intact or broken.

A person may feel the bone break or hear it snap. Pain and tenderness are almost always present. Usually there is total or partial impairment of function of the affected part. For example, anyone whose leg is so injured that he cannot walk should be suspected of having a broken bone. In addition to swelling or bruising around the fracture site, there may also be a deformity or odd appearance.

What to Do for a Closed Fracture (Skin Not Broken)

1. Do not move the injured person or the injured part until the suspected fracture has been placed in a splint.

2. Call a doctor right away.

3. If a doctor's services will be immediately available, nothing need be done except to make the victim as comfortable as possible by keeping him warm and placing something soft under his head, except in suspected neck injuries.

4. If a doctor is not immediately available, many important things should be done:

  a. Look for and treat any bleeding areas (pp. 30-33).
  b. **Gently** remove or cut away clothing from the injured part.
  c. Apply a splint to the injured extremity.

SPLINTING

Splinting is the application of any material or apparatus to an injured part in order to keep it motionless, and thus prevent further injury and pain.

An injured leg can be adequately immobilized by bandaging it to the well leg—or an extremity can be bound into a pillow or blanket reinforced on two or three sides by pieces of wood or such rigid objects as a metal rod, pole, broomstick, mop handle, cane, baseball bat, rolled-up magazine, or thick folded newspaper. A splint should be long enough to extend well beyond the joints above and below the fracture.

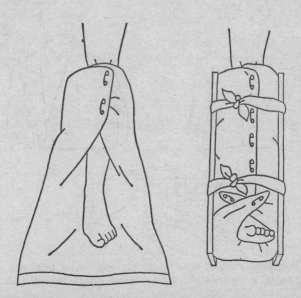

Use clothing or soft material to pad the splint, preventing injury to the skin and further discomfort. Secure the splint with strips of clothing or sheets in at least three places—beyond the joints on either side of the fracture, and halfway between them.

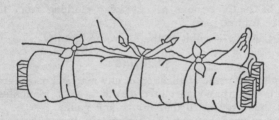

Fractures in the hand, wrist, forearm, ankle, or foot can be immobilized with a pillow or blanket bound around them. A wooden tongue blade may be used to splint a broken finger.

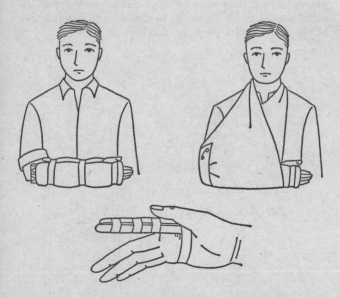

Recently a new type of splint has come into use. Made of a lightweight, transparent plastic which can be inflated by mouth like a balloon in a matter of seconds, it can be stored in a small space. This makes it suitable for use at home, in a car, on a boat, or wherever first-aid equipment is kept.

If no splinting material is available, you may splint a broken finger or toe by bandaging it to an adjacent uninjured digit.

What to Do for an Open Fracture (Skin Broken)

1. **Gently** remove or cut away clothing from the injured part.

2. Place a sterile gauze pad or a clean handkerchief or part of a clean sheet, shirt, or towel over the wound and press firmly with your hand to control any bleeding.

3. Then secure the pad with a strong bandage, using a necktie, scarf, handkerchief, or gauze.

4. If you cannot provide a pad or bandage to cover the wound and it is still bleeding, close the wound with your hand or fingers and apply pressure directly over the wound.

5. Call a doctor as soon as the bleeding is under control.

6. If a doctor's services will be immediately available, nothing more need be done except to make the victim as comfortable as possible by keeping him warm and placing something soft under his head, except in suspected neck injuries.

7. If a doctor is not immediately available, apply a splint to the injured part as outlined in the procedure for closed fractures on pp. 77-79.

FRACTURES OF THE FACIAL BONES AND NOSE

No special first-aid treatment is necessary for fractures or suspected fractures of this type. However, in order to correct any possible deformities which might have functional or cosmetic consequences, the person should be seen by a doctor shortly following the injury.

FRACTURES OF THE JAWS

Fractures of the upper and lower jaws generally do not require first aid **unless there is interference with breathing or severe bleeding.** If breathing is being interfered with, place the victim on his side and gently pull the front part of the lower jaw forward. Severe bleeding usually can be controlled by placing a piece of sterile gauze against the bleeding area and pressing gently but firmly.

All suspected fractures of the upper and lower jaws should be seen by a physician or oral surgeon as soon as possible because improper healing of a jaw fracture will result in incorrect alignment of the teeth. Until the patient with a suspected fracture obtains professional help, immobilize the jaw and support it with a chin bandage. Fold a large handkerchief into a triangle and then into a band about three inches wide; draw it under the chin and tie it tightly on the top of the head.

FRACTURES OF THE COLLARBONE

These are a common occurrence in childhood, and at any age are usually the result of a direct blow or a fall upon an outstretched arm. Although they are generally considered minor injuries, your doctor should be called right away. In addition to pain, swelling, tender-

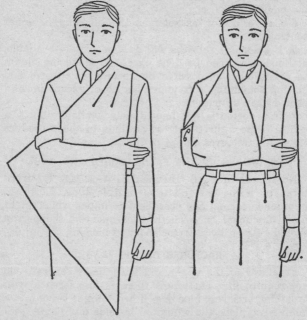

ness, and disability, the break may also produce deformity or an odd appearance, which makes the injury easy to recognize.

What to Do

Place the arm on the affected side in a triangular bandage sling. The victim should hold his shoulders as far back as possible to lessen the pain. He should be seen by a physician, who may then apply a special bandage which keeps the shoulders in the best position for healing.

FRACTURES OF THE RIBS

Rib fractures are very common, resulting from falls and blows. In addition, they may sometimes occur from coughing or sneezing. They almost always produce sharp pain which is made worse by breathing, coughing, or laughing. There is usually tenderness, but rarely swelling or deformity.

Because of the pain and possible damage to the underlying lung, suspected rib fractures should be seen by a physician. He should be called right away if there is any coughing up of blood following a chest injury, as this may indicate a broken rib has penetrated a lung.

FRACTURES OF THE PELVIS

Since the pelvic bones are extremely strong and generally well padded, they are rarely fractured except in severe accidents—and then a doctor should be called immediately. Pelvic fractures can be serious because there may be injury to the bladder, bowel, rectum, vagina, or large arteries. Be prepared to treat for possible shock (pp. 34-35).

In suspected fractures of the pelvis the victim should be kept lying down and as motionless as possible. Do not move him until a doctor or ambulance arrives on the scene.

— 10 —

MUSCLE AND JOINT INJURIES

DISLOCATIONS

A dislocation results when a force dislodges a bone out of its position in the joint. Although dislocations may occur in any joint, the fingers, thumbs, and shoulders are most frequently affected. The ligaments surrounding the joint are torn or loosened in the process of dislocation. The symptoms are similar to those of a fracture —pain, swelling, tenderness, impairment of joint function, and often a prominent deformity or odd appearance.

What to Do

1. The treatment is the same as for a closed fracture (pp. 77-79). Chiefly, this means keeping the injured part motionless until medical attention is obtained.

2. A splint is not needed for dislocation of fingers or thumbs, since they can be kept immobilized by the patient himself until he is seen by a doctor.

3. Use an arm sling for a shoulder dislocation. Do not attempt to reposition a dislocated shoulder yourself, as this may cause further damage of a serious nature.

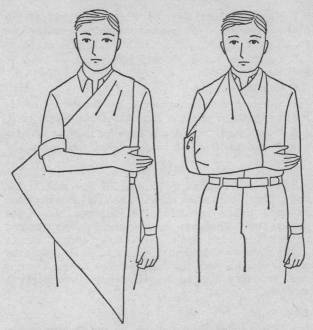

4. If the dislocation occurs in the hip, the person should not be allowed to walk.

SPRAINS

Sprains are injuries to ligaments and tendons surrounding joints. They occur when the joint is forced into motion beyond its usual range. The most common sprain is that of the ankle—with knees, wrists, and fingers next in frequency. Sprains result in pain (aggravated by motion), swelling, tenderness, and sometimes discoloration. Since these signs are also produced by fractures, one cannot always distinguish sprains from fractures. They may, in fact, both be present, and if the doctor suspects a fracture, he will want to have X rays taken.

What to Do

1. If there is any possibility of fracture, immobilize or splint the part as described for a closed fracture (pp. 77-79).

2. Keep the part elevated above the level of the heart, if possible. This position minimizes swelling and pain.

3. Apply ice packs or cold compresses as soon as possible.

4. Call your doctor.

5. A person with a sprained ankle should not be allowed to walk or stand or otherwise bear weight on it.

6. Do not apply heat in any form for the first twenty-four hours, as it can increase swelling and pain.

STRAINS

Strains are injuries to muscles in any part of the body. They occur when muscle fibers are overstretched or torn, usually by sudden or improper use of the muscle itself. They are the so-called "pulled tendons" in the calf or thigh, also called "Charley horses." Strains result in pain which is mild, except when the particular muscle is used—then the pain becomes severe. There is some disability, little tenderness, rarely discoloration or swelling.

What to Do

1. The strained muscle should be rested. This can be assured by not allowing movement of the affected parts, avoiding any movement that is painful.

2. Apply an electric heating pad or a hot water bottle —unless you think you have torn a muscle in your calf. In this case, you should apply an ice pack to minimize hemorrhage and swelling in the leg.

3. Call your doctor.

ACUTE LOW BACK PAIN

Most acute backaches are due to acute muscle strain. They may be brought on by some sudden or unexpected movement, lifting, pushing, bending forward to pick something up, or remaining in an awkward position for some length of time.

Of course, there is a possibility that the backache is being caused by a "slipped disc," especially if there is pain down the back of one or both legs (sometimes called sciatica or sciatic pain). Your doctor's examination will help to determine whether the symptoms are due to the much more common low back strain, or to an intervertebral disc. In either case, the following is the correct first-aid treatment.

What to Do

1. Have the person lie down on a hard surface like a floor rather than on a soft bed.

2. Knees and hips bent is usually the position of greatest comfort.

3. Place an electric heating pad or a hot water bottle under the area of maximum discomfort, being careful not to burn the skin.

4. Call your doctor.

Prevention

1. Never try to lift a heavy object quickly or suddenly.

2. When bending down to pick up something from the floor, or when lifting a heavy object, keep the entire back vertical and bend with your hips, knees, and ankles.

3. Do not lift a heavy weight in front of you above the waistline.

4. When trying to raise a hard-to-open window, stand close to it and keep your back straight up and down. Use your hands, arms, and legs—not your back—for leverage.

5. Never bend backward.

6. Avoid remaining with your back in a tense or unnatural position for any length of time.

SEVERE MUSCLE CRAMPS

Although not due to external injury, muscle cramps can be very painful, occurring primarily in the calves and feet. They are rare in children, infrequent in young adults, and increasingly common as people get older. They may come on during exercise, but develop more frequently during rest, especially at night and in the early morning hours. Stretching may also bring them on.

Contrary to popular belief, muscle cramps are not a reliable sign of faulty circulation. In the summer or in very hot climates they may be an indication of deficient salt intake.

What to Do

1. Gently massage the affected muscle until the painful contraction is relieved.

2. Apply a hot water bottle or electric heating pad.

3. If you get these cramps more than a few times in a matter of a month, consult your physician, as he may give you more specific advice or medication to prevent their recurrence.

– 11 –

BURNS

Burns rank second as the cause of death in home accidents. Every year in the United States more than six thousand people die from fires occurring in the home. For every fatality there are estimated to be a hundred serious injuries, totaling some six hundred thousand annually.

Types of Burns

The great majority of burns result from the direct effect of heat and are called thermal burns. Burns may also be caused by chemicals, electricity, too much sun or ultraviolet light, and X rays. These different forms of energy produce burns of varying **degrees**, depending upon the amount of skin irritation or destruction.

First-degree burns produce only reddening of the skin.

Second-degree burns produce blisters as well as reddening of the skin.

Third-degree burns produce still deeper destruction, damaging the entire skin thickness and varying amounts of tissues beneath the skin.

What to Do for Extensive or Serious Burns Due to Heat or Fire (Thermal Burns)

1. Call your doctor immediately.
2. Have the victim lie down.

3. Place sterile dressings (or the cleanest available cloth material such as part of a sheet or shirt or a freshly ironed handkerchief) over all the burned areas to keep air out.

4. Do not break the blisters or try to clean the burn.

5. Keep the patient quiet and comfortably warm until the doctor comes.

What to Do for Small or Mild Burns Due to Heat or Fire (Thermal Burns)

1. Place the burned part under cold running water or immerse it in clean, cold water for two to three minutes.

2. Do not disturb or open any blisters.

3. Apply petroleum jelly, butter, or cold cream liberally to the burn or to a sterile gauze pad (or the cleanest available cloth material such as part of a sheet or shirt or a freshly ironed handkerchief) and cover the burned part.

4. Secure the dressing with gauze or adhesive tape.

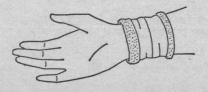

What to Do for Chemical Burns

1. Immediately wash with large amounts of cold running water (in **carbolic acid** burns first irrigate with rubbing or drinking alcohol and then wash with water).

2. Remove any clothing soaked with the chemical.

3. Place sterile dressings (or the cleanest available cloth material such as part of a sheet or shirt or a freshly ironed handkerchief) over all the burned areas to keep air out.

4. If first-aid directions against the specific chemical are available on the label of the container, follow them. Otherwise, do not apply any chemical to the burned area.

5. Do not disturb or open any blisters.

Common causes of chemical burns are:

CARBOLIC ACID	LIME
CAUSTIC POTASH	NITRIC ACID
CAUSTIC SODA	SULFURIC ACID
HYDROCHLORIC ACID	

ELECTRICAL BURNS

Burns of this nature may follow contact with a charged electric wire or an electrical apparatus. They may also result from being hit by a bolt of lightning. **First aid must be given immediately.**

What to Do

1. If there is a third person on the scene, have him call for medical help.

2. Do not touch the victim until he is separated from the current.

a. Wherever possible, turn off the electric power.

b. Pull the person from the electrical contact using any dry nonconductor such as rope, a leather belt, a wooden pole or board, a coat, or a loop of cloth either to remove the wire from the victim without touching the wire—or to remove the victim from the wire without touching him.

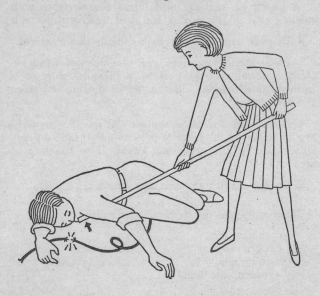

3. Once the victim is separated from the current, and **if he has stopped breathing, begin mouth-to-mouth breathing** (pp. 23-29) and continue until medical help arrives—even though the victim may appear to be lifeless. (Many electric shock victims thought to be dead have been revived after several hours of this kind of resuscitation.)

4. Once the victim is separated from the current, and **if he is breathing regularly,** keep him lying down, loosen the clothing around his neck, and call a doctor.

5. Place sterile dressings (or the cleanest available cloth material such as part of a sheet or shirt or a freshly ironed handkerchief) over the burned area to keep the air out.

6. Do not try to clean the burn or disturb the blisters.

7. Keep the patient quiet and comfortably warm until the doctor comes.

SUNBURN

People vary greatly in their reaction and sensitivity to ultraviolet rays from the sun or artificial sources such as sun lamps. Blonds and redheads are generally more susceptible than brunettes, and infants more sensitive than adults.

What to Do

1. For mild sunburn, the application of cold cream or such greases or oils as shortening or salad oil may relieve the pain.

2. If blistering appears, apply petroleum jelly or cold cream to sterile gauze dressings (or the cleanest available cloth material such as part of a sheet or shirt or a freshly ironed handkerchief) and cover the area.

3. Always call a doctor in extensive or severe cases of sunburn—or when there are accompanying chills, nausea, or vomiting.

4. Do **not** expose any sunburned area to the sun again until the burn is completely healed.

Prevention

The best preventive measure against sunburn is limiting the time of your initial exposure. Your first time out should not be longer than five to thirty minutes, depending upon your skin coloring, general sensitivity, the time of day, and the season of the year.

Extensive or severe sunburn is especially likely to occur on water or at the beach, even on an overcast or cloudy day. High altitudes and reflection of the sun's rays by sand, snow, and ice also increase the intensity of exposure.

IN CASE OF FIRE

Every family should have a plan of action and escape in the event of a fire. There are certain fundamental rules that apply in most cases:

1. The air from the floor is mostly smoke-free, so crawl on the floor if the room is filled with smoke.

2. Close doors, windows, and transoms to prevent the fire from spreading. If you are awaiting rescue, however, and are near a window, open it slightly and breathe the incoming air.

3. It is especially important to protect your breathing passages, face, and hands. Tying a wet handkerchief or other thin cloth over the nose and mouth will keep out some of the smoke and burning-hot air. (More people die from the suffocating effects of fire than from skin burns).

4. A thick fabric or material, when wet, offers protection to the part of the body it covers.

5. If you are alone and your clothes are on fire, lie down at once and slowly roll over back and forth. If another person's clothing is on fire, have him lie down at once and try to smother the flames using a coat, rug, or blanket.

6. Jumping from upper-story windows or roofs is very hazardous, potentially fatal, and often unnecessary, as fire trucks with ladders and nets are usually on the scene within a few minutes.

HOME FIRE PREVENTION

Most fires in the home show evidence of some human failure or some careless act. So make these safety rules a permanent part of your everyday life.

1. Don't smoke in bed or when you are sleepy—or under the influence of sedatives or alcohol.

2. Don't use inflammable cleaning fluids near an open flame or while smoking.

3. Don't pour inflammable liquids into a coal or wood stove or a fireplace.

4. Don't attempt to find a leaking gas pipe with an open flame light.

5. Don't leave on any electrical appliance, such as an iron, after use.

6. Don't let trash accumulate anywhere around the house, as it can cause spontaneous combustion.

7. Don't overload electrical circuits.

8. Store inflammable materials in a safe place.

9. Hang clothes well away from stoves or fireplaces.

10. Make sure that curtains and draperies are not hung where they may blow into or near flames.

11. Be extremely cautious whenever lighted candles are used.

12. Don't use wastebaskets as ash trays. Keep plenty of ash trays around every room of the house.

13. Provide adequate guards for fireplaces.

14. When building or buying a home, seek informa-

15. Never leave an outside fire unattended, as when tion as to its fire safety. Older homes should be checked periodically for defective or inadequate wiring—also heating systems and electrical equipment.

15. Never leave an outside fire unattended, as when burning leaves or rubbish. Be sure that your fire site is far enough away from trees or wooden structures so the fire does not spread. Before you leave the fire site, make certain that the fire is completely out and there is no smoke coming from it.

Prevention of Burns in Children

Since children are so frequently injured or killed by fire (nearly 30 per cent of all victims are children), the following rules should be applied in every home:

1. Don't hold a baby or small child while you are smoking or while drinking hot liquids.

2. Don't let small children put their hands into hot food.

3. Don't allow small children in the kitchen, if at all possible, and if you do, keep pot handles turned away from the edge of the stove or sink.

4. Don't allow small children in the laundry, if at all possible, and if you do, see that they are kept away from pails, sinks, and tubs filled with hot water.

5. Keep tablecloths, runners, and scarves from hanging over the sides of tables or other furniture on which you might place steaming hot liquids such as coffee or tea.

6. Keep matches stored in a metal container out of the reach of children. Use safety matches only. Don't let children play with cigarette lighters.

7. Keep children away from stoves, gas and electric heaters, and radiators.

8. Never let a child play around an open fire without supervision.

9. When bathing a small child, place him facing the tub faucets so he will not back up against the hot water faucet accidentally. See that he keeps his hands off the faucets, as a child can be badly scalded by a burst of hot water.

10. When the child is old enough, show him the correct way to strike a match and teach him the right way to handle fire.

11. Occasionally conduct family discussions on fire prevention, burn prevention, home safety, and what to do in case of fire.

— 12 —

ELECTRIC SHOCK

The widespread use and availability of electric power has produced countless potential hazards that can lead to accidental electrocution or lesser degrees of bodily injury. Nature's own unharnessed electricity—lightning —claims four hundred human lives and causes approximately one thousand cases of injuries every year in the United States.

First aid must be given immediately to save a victim of electric shock.

What to Do for Electric Power Shock

1. If there is a third person on the scene, have him call for medical help.

2. Do not touch the victim until he is separated from the current.

    a. Wherever possible, turn off the electric power.

    b. Pull the person from the electrical contact using any dry nonconductor such as rope, a leather belt, a wooden pole or board, a coat, or a loop of cloth either to remove the wire from the victim without touching the wire—or to remove the victim from the wire without touching him.

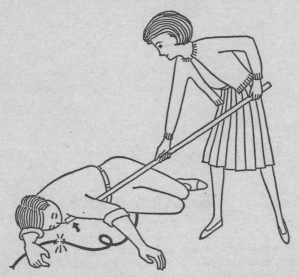

3. Once the victim is separated from the current, and **if he has stopped breathing, begin mouth-to-mouth breathing** (pp. 23-29) and continue until medical help arrives—even though the victim may appear to be lifeless. (Many electric shock victims thought to be dead have been revived after several hours of this kind of resuscitation.)

4. Once the victim is separated from the current, and **if he is breathing regularly,** keep him lying down, loosen the clothing around his neck, and **call a doctor,** if one is not already on the way.

What to Do for Lightning Shock

1. If there is a third person on the scene, have him call for medical help.

2. If the victim has stopped breathing, begin mouth-to-mouth breathing (pp. 23-29) and continue until medical help arrives—even though the victim may appear to be lifeless. (Many electric shock victims thought to be dead have been revived after several hours of this kind of resuscitation.)

3. If he is breathing regularly, keep him lying down, loosen the clothing around his neck, and **call a doctor,** if one is not already on the way.

Prevention

Children, especially during their exploratory years, are easy victims of electric shock. Seal all electrical outlets which are within the reach of children, using adhesive tape or special safety plugs manufactured for this purpose. Wall outlets are dangerous because youngsters frequently stick pins, nails, or other metallic objects into them, resulting in sometimes fatal accidents.

Adults should remember not to touch any electrical equipment if body, hands, or feet are wet. Most electrical appliances, unless very specifically certified, should *never* be used in the bathroom.

The greatest number of lightning accidents occur in rural or open areas. Campers, golfers, swimmers, and boaters are the most vulnerable. **If you are out in the open** when a thunderstorm develops, **head for a building** and remain inside until the storm is over. **If you are swimming or boating, leave the water** and get to a building. If no building is available, head for a grove of trees, but **avoid a lone tree.** In a completely open area, lie down flat on the ground until the storm passes.

If you are at the top of a mountain, get to a lower elevation as soon as possible. **If you are driving** in a closed automobile (an all-steel car affords protection, a convertible does not), it is wise to **pull off the road** and wait for the storm to abate, but **keep away from trees. If you are at home, stay away from open doors and windows.** Refrain from bathing or using the telephone or any electrical appliance until the storm is over.

– 13 –

DROWNING

Drowning, which accounts for one out of every fifteen fatal accidents in the United States, is the fourth leading cause of accidental deaths in all age groups. Every year the death toll from drowning numbers between six and seven thousand victims—50 per cent being between the ages of five and twenty-four.

The best single insurance against drowning is learning how to swim properly. Approximately one hundred million persons participate in some form of water activity each year in the United States. Almost half are unable to pass the Red Cross Beginner's Test for swimming, and probably would be unable to save themselves from drowning.

As forty million Americans take to the water annually in eight million boats, the risk of drowning increases; so does the necessity for proper boating safety programs. *It is essential for everyone to know the rules of water safety and rescue.* In addition to boating and fishing, more people are engaging in more active water sports than ever before—water skiing, diving, riding the surf, and exploring the mysteries of underwater life by skin and scuba diving. Swimming pools in the nation now number two hundred and fifty thousand.

Drowning can also occur right in your own home. Remember these two home safety rules: **1) Never leave a small child unattended in a bathtub, even for a second, for any reason,** and **2) Never bathe while under the influence of sleeping pills or other sedation.** Adults have been known to drown in just a few inches of water.

What to Do in the Water

(Not everyone can or should follow the detailed instructions in this section. You should be a good swimmer, preferably with some knowledge of rescue techniques, before attempting to save a drowning person in the water. Do not become a victim yourself.)

1. If the victim is not breathing, begin mouth-to-mouth breathing (pp. 23-29) **immediately.** Rescue breathing must be started as soon as you can reach the victim's mouth or nose with your mouth.

2. Grasp the top of the victim's head with one hand, tilting the head far back. (This usually opens the mouth.) Keep the head in this position. Your other hand or arm should be placed across the victim's chest and locked in his armpit to support his body.

3. The first ten breaths should be given as fast as possible. Don't be concerned if the first few breaths cause water to spurt from the victim's nose and mouth. As you carry him ashore, **breathe for him at least once every ten seconds.**

4. If he does not recover breathing by the time you reach shore, don't struggle to get him out of the water. Leave him in shallow water as you continue to breathe for him. Cool water will reduce his need for oxygen. In addition, in shallow water he will be easier to pick up by stretcher or by hand when help arrives.

5. You can kneel in the water and rest his head on your knee, keeping him afloat. Now you are able to use both hands to hold his head tilted back fully and his chin pulled forward. This position also enables you to switch from mouth-to-mouth to mouth-to-nose breathing if too much air is being blown into his stomach.

6. When the victim begins to recover, get him ashore so you can take better care of him if there are complications. If he vomits food or sea water, keep his head lower than his chest, if possible, and turn his head to one side. This will allow the material to flow out of his mouth and not into his lungs. Try to clear his throat of mucus, vomitus, or water with your fingers.

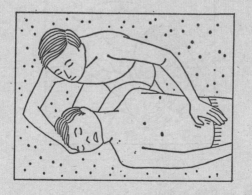

7. If the victim has a convulsive seizure during re-covery, give him **mouth-to-nose** breathing.

8. If he lapses back to shallow breathing or turns bluish in color, breathe mouth-to-mouth in rhythm with him. He may need mouth-to-mouth breathing even in the ambulance. Continue to breathe for him until medical help takes over.

What to Do from a Boat

1. In deep water, you can begin rescue breathing as soon as you reach the victim. **Approach him stern-first** to avoid capsizing your boat.

2. It is essential to **hold his body securely.** With the victim facing you, hook either your right arm through his right armpit or your left arm through his left armpit. With this lock grip, you can hold his head tilted way back with your other hand on the top of his head. His mouth will open if you tilt his head enough, thereby making it easy to give him mouth-to-mouth breathing (pp. 23-29). To avoid fatiguing yourself, lower him a little between breaths, as the water will help to buoy him.

3. Give him five minutes of rescue breathing before worrying about getting him into the boat or ashore. The chances are that if you have reached him in time, he will recover promptly. Many victims of water submersion have been saved after only three minutes of rescue breathing.

What to Do Once on Land

Don't waste time in attempting to empty water out of the victim by pumping or inverting him. (A ten-second delay can mean the difference between life and death. Water may have been swallowed but this does no harm. Only a small fraction of the water which has been breathed in can be "poured out.") **If the victim is not breathing, begin mouth-to-mouth or mouth-to-nose breathing (pp. 23-29) immediately.**

— 14 —

DIVING INJURIES

The cardinal rule of first aid for victims of driving accidents also applies to victims of diving accidents—"Don't move the patient." The fear of the victim's drowning leads many untrained rescuers to remove the person from the water, but this is extremely dangerous as a spinal injury at the neck is more likely to occur in a diving accident than in a traffic accident.

What to Do

1. Keep the victim in the water until trained help arrives on the scene with a spine board or taut stretcher. Water makes an excellent support for the patient, who can easily be kept afloat with hand support. It is important to maintain his head and neck in a position level with his back.

2. If needed, mouth-to-mouth breathing (pp. 23-29) can be done while the patient is floating in the water.

3. If there is excessive bleeding or if the water is too cold to allow the victim to remain in it, he should be removed with the help of a rigid support such as a wooden plank, a surfboard, or a door.

— 15 —

HEAT EXHAUSTION AND

HEATSTROKE

HEAT EXHAUSTION (HEAT COLLAPSE OR HEAT PROSTRATION)

Heat exhaustion occurs when a person has been exposed to high temperatures for a long enough period to cause him to lose important body fluids and salt. This produces a fall in blood pressure and impairs the brain's blood supply.

Symptoms and Signs

The victim is frequently listless, apprehensive, pale, has clammy skin, and a rapid and weak pulse. He may suffer from weakness, headache, dizziness, dim or blurred vision, cramps in the abdomen or limbs, nausea, and vomiting. In extreme cases, the person may collapse completely and go into a near coma or unconsciousness.

What to Do

1. Have the victim lie down flat, preferably with his head lower than his body.

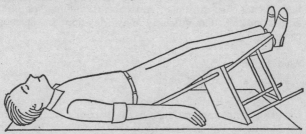

2. Loosen any tight clothing.

3. Move him as soon as possible to a cool place, but be careful that he does not get chilled.

4. If the person is conscious, give him cool salt water to drink (one half teaspoon salt to one half glass of water).

5. Call a doctor.

6. Offer the victim one half glass salt water every fifteen minutes unless the doctor gives other instructions.

Prevention

In extremely hot weather, it is important to:

1. Avoid undue exertion.

2. Dress in lightweight, loose-fitting clothing.

3. Unless you have been previously told to restrict your salt or sodium intake, take two salt tablets with each glass of water you drink every time you are thirsty.

HEATSTROKE (OR SUNSTROKE)

Anyone who has been exposed to heat or the direct rays of a hot sun for one to several hours, and then develops a temperature of 100 degrees or more, should be suspected of coming down with heatstroke—unless the fever can be otherwise explained. Heatstroke is a potentially serious condition needing **immediate medical attention.**

Symptoms and Signs

The victim looks flushed and his skin is *hot* and *dry,* his pulse rapid and strong. He may suffer from weakness, headache, dizziness, muscular twitching, nausea, and vomiting. Convulsions may develop in serious cases.

What to Do

1. Call a doctor at once.

2. Cool the body by sponging it with cold water or by using cold applications. If the victim's temperature by mouth is 102 degrees or more, place him in a tub of cold or iced water and check his temperature every half hour until it is under 102 degrees.

3. If the person is fully conscious and can swallow, give him cool salt water to drink (one teaspoon salt to one quart of water)—or plain cold or iced water.

4. Do not give the victim alcohol in any form.

5. If convulsions develop, treat as described on pp. 169-170.

Prevention

1. Wear a hat with a brim wide enough to prevent direct heating of the head.

2. Avoid undue exertion in extremely hot weather.

— 16 —

FROSTBITE

Frostbite is actual freezing of the skin and possibly deeper tissues due to exposure to air temperature below freezing. Minor degrees of frostbite are quite common, usually affecting the ears, nose, toes or fingers. In sub-zero temperatures frostbite can occur in a matter of minutes. Prevention can be accomplished in all kinds of weather by proper clothing and insulation.

Signs of Frostbite

Next to prevention, early recognition is of the greatest importance. The affected skin usually becomes pink, begins to tingle, then may become numb and frosty white in appearance. There is usually little or no pain because the rapid freezing produces loss of sensation. This is why the victim may not be aware that he has been frostbitten.

What to Do

1. Bring the victim indoors as soon as possible.

2. Cover the frostbitten part with a warm hand or woolen material. If the fingers or hand are frostbitten, have the person hold his hand in his armpit, next to his body.

3. Place the frostbitten part in lukewarm water.

4. Gently wrap the part in blankets if lukewarm water is not available or is impractical to use.

5. Call a doctor.

6. Let the circulation re-establish itself naturally.

7. When the part is warmed, encourage the victim to exercise his fingers and toes.

8. Give the person a warm, **nonalcoholic** drink.

Do not rub the skin with snow or ice. Rubbing frost-bitten tissue increases the risk of gangrene.

Do not use hot water, hot water bottles, or heat lamps over the frostbitten area.

— 17 —

SWALLOWED FOREIGN BODIES

Any object which fits into the mouth and can be swallowed is usually able to reach the stomach and continue through the intestinal tract and then be eliminated through the rectum.

Common round, smooth objects such as coins, marbles, pebbles, rings, and buttons are almost always harmless. Even sharp objects such as open safety pins, nails, and glass fragments will frequently pass through the entire intestinal tract without producing serious harm.

What to Do

There is no need for emergency treatment in the care of children or adults who have swallowed a foreign body. **Cathartics or laxatives must not be given under any circumstances.**

Keep calm and call your doctor for further advice.

— 18 —

BITES AND STINGS

STINGING INSECTS

(Bees, Wasps, Hornets, Yellow Jackets)

While stinging insects have long been feared because of the pain they inflict, recent attention has been focused on the fact that they can cause fatalities—accounting for as many deaths annually in the United States as snakes and all other venomous creatures put together.

Some fatalities are the result of a single sting; others are due to multiple stings. These deaths usually occur in people who have previously experienced a profound or severe allergic reaction to the same kind of insect sting.

A person known to be allergic to the venom of a specific insect should consult a physician, since preventive medical treatment is available to help make that individual more resistant to the effects of the insect sting. In certain cases, this treatment can be lifesaving.

What to Do for a Person with NO KNOWN Allergy to the Insect Sting

1. Apply an ice pack or cold cloths to the affected area.

2. Remove the stinger by gently scraping it out with the tip of a sharp knife. If one is not available, use your fingernail. Do **not** use tweezers or fingers to grasp the stinger, as this may squeeze more venom into the sting.

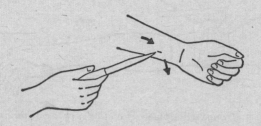

3. Mix two teaspoons of household ammonia **or** two teaspoons of baking soda (or bicarbonate of soda) in a glass of water. Pour this solution on cotton and use as a moist dressing.

4. If you have been stung in many places, get into a lukewarm bath to which you should add a small package of baking soda (or bicarbonate of soda).

5. Call your doctor.

6. **Do not** apply mud packs.

7. **Do not** scratch any sting, for scratching may introduce an infection.

What to Do for a Person with
A KNOWN Allergy to the Insect Sting

1. If there is a third person on the scene, have him call for medical help.

2. Make the person lie down at once—if possible, with his head below the level of his heart, and his legs elevated.

3. If the sting is on an extremity (feet, legs, hands, or arms), apply a constricting band or tourniquet (see illustrations) two to four inches closer to the heart than the site of the sting.

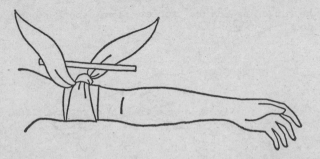

Wrap a strong, wide piece of cloth (such as a handkerchief or necktie) twice around the arm or leg and tie a half knot. Place a short stick (or similar object such as a ruler) on the half knot and . . .

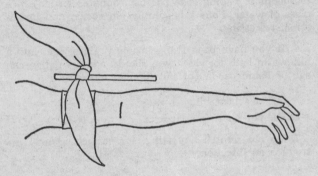

. . . tie a square knot.

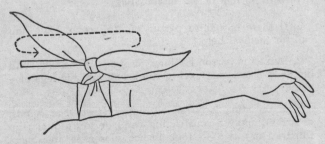

Twist the stick to tighten the tourniquet.

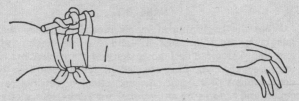

Hold the stick in place with the end of the tourniquet or another strip of cloth.

4. The constricting band or tourniquet should be tightened slightly. This will usually make the arm or leg bluish in color and make the veins stand out. **It should not be so tight that the arm or leg is white.** If you know where the body pulses can be felt, check to see that a pulse is present below the constricting band or tourniquet.

5. Loosen the constricting band or tourniquet for a few seconds every fifteen minutes until the person is under medical supervision.

6. Place an ice pack or cold cloths to the affected area.

7. Begin mouth-to-mouth breathing (pp. 23-29) if the person's breathing is very weak, or if his lips or fingernails are bluish in color.

8. Remove the stinger by gently scraping it out with the tip of a sharp knife. If one is not available, use your fingernail. Do **not** use tweezers or fingers to grasp the stinger, as this may squeeze more venom into the sting.

9. Call your doctor as soon as possible, unless he has already been called and is on his way.

What NOT to Do

1. Do not let the victim walk.

2. Do not use any narrow material such as rope, twine, or wire for the constricting band or tourniquet.

3. Do not conceal the constricting band or tourniquet —in this way you and others are reminded that it is there and needs to be loosened every fifteen minutes.

4. Do not give the person alcohol in any form.

5. Do not apply mud packs.

SNAKE BITE

From the beginning of man's recorded history there has been much interest in—and fear of—snake bites and their effects. The high toxicity of many venoms has long been known. This has led in recent years to the development of several new and effective serums (also called antivenoms or antivenins) for snake bite victims.

Fortunately, the great majority of snakes in the United States are non-poisonous. The poisonous snakes are either pit vipers or coral snakes.

Pit vipers have a hollow or pit on each side of the head between the eye and the nostril. The pit vipers include the *water moccasin or cottonmouth* (so called because the inside of the mouth is white), the *copperhead or highland moccasin,* and the thirteen species of *rattlesnake,* known by its rattles.

There are two species of *coral snakes* in the United States, one in the Southeast and the other in southern Arizona. Brilliantly colored with bands of red, yellow, and black, coral snakes are sluggish and do not strike like pit vipers, but bite if stepped on or handled. They resemble certain harmless snakes, but can be identified by their black snouts and the colored bands that extend right across their bellies.

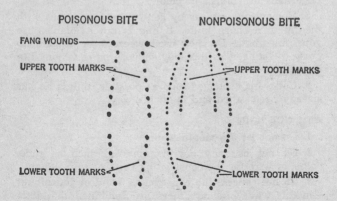

POISONOUS BITE   NONPOISONOUS BITE

FANG WOUNDS

UPPER TOOTH MARKS   UPPER TOOTH MARKS

LOWER TOOTH MARKS   LOWER TOOTH MARKS

Most bites from pit vipers bring immediate and severe pain, swelling, and discoloration. Coral snake venom produces only slight burning pain and mild swelling.

Bites from non-poisonous snakes give little pain or swelling beyond what is usual for any wound.

Immediate and proper first aid can be lifesaving. Many people bitten by snakes become excited, hysterical, and panicky, even if the bite came from a non-poisonous snake. Such excitement and panic can complicate and aggravate the victim's condition, and should, therefore, be alleviated as much as possible by reassurance. Remember—*extremely few victims die* or become permanently disabled from snake bite when first aid has been administered promptly and correctly.

What to Do

If the snake is positively identified as a *non-poisonous* species, clean the wound with soap and water or an antiseptic and report to a doctor as soon as possible.

If the snake is definitely identified as a **poisonous** species or is unidentified, do the following:

1. Kill the snake immediately, if possible, and keep it. Its identity is necessary before specific antivenom treatment can be given. Most snakes can be killed with one sharp blow to the head. However, do not spend more than a few moments in this activity or move more than a few feet from the spot where the bite occurred.

2. Make the victim lie down at once.

3. Keep the bitten part still and in a position below the level of the heart. The victim should be kept dry and warm and not allowed to walk around. Any fear or excitement should be counteracted by reassurance that snake bite is very rarely fatal.

4. Never give alcohol to a snake bite victim.

5. If the bite is on an extremity (feet, legs, hands, or arms), apply a constricting band or tourniquet (pp. 114-115) two to four inches closer to the heart than the site of the bite. If swelling progresses up the arm or leg, replace the constricting band or tourniquet closer to the heart than the swelling.

6. The constricting band or tourniquet should be tightened slightly. This will usually make the arm or leg bluish in color and make the veins stand out. It may also cause the bite to ooze. **It should not be so**

tight that the arm or leg is white. If you know where the body pulses can be felt, check to see that a pulse is present below the constricting band or tourniquet.

7. Loosen the constricting band or tourniquet for a few seconds every fifteen minutes until the victim is under medical supervision.

8. Place an ice pack, if possible, directly over the bite, wherever the bite is located.

9. Call your doctor. If you are not near a telephone, carry the victim (pp. 41-48) to the nearest doctor or hospital for further treatment such as suction, incision, and the administration of antivenom.

What NOT to Do

1. Do not let the victim walk.

2. Do not give him alcohol of any kind.

3. Do not use any narrow material such as rope, twine, or wire for the constricting band or tourniquet.

4. **Do not conceal the constricting band or tourniquet** —in this way you and others are reminded that it is there and needs to be loosened every fifteen minutes.

5. Do not use so-called "snake bite" remedies.

Precautions to Take in Snake-Infested Areas

1. Don't walk about at twilight, during the night, and shortly after sunrise, if possible. Snakes in general, and poisonous types in particular, become more active during the night.

2. Don't swim in areas where you know snakes abound, for a bite from a poisonous snake inflicted in the water is just as dangerous as on land.

3. Don't place your hands, whether wearing gloves or not, on rocky ledges, in hollow logs, under boards or planks, or near any place where a snake might be hidden from view.

4. Don't step into such places with bare feet or while wearing sandals. Wear thick leather boots, as more than half of all snake bites occur below the calf of the leg.

5. Don't sit down in areas possibly infested with snakes until you have taken a careful look around.

6. Don't camp near piles of brush, rocks, or other debris.

7. Don't sleep on the ground if you can possibly avoid it.

8. Don't step over a log or rock, even during daylight hours, without examining what is on the other side.

9. Don't gather firewood or other objects at night when you cannot clearly see where you step or reach.

10. Don't walk close to rock walls or ledges. Stay a few feet away or inspect carefully as you walk.

11. Don't hike alone, for in the event of a bite it is essential to have at least one person along to perform vital first aid and to catch, kill, or identify the snake.

12. Don't handle a poisonous snake that has just been killed—always use a stick or other means to manipulate it, as it still can, by reflex action, inflict a dangerous bite.

13. Don't ever pick up a snake unless it is absolutely necessary, or without knowing positively that it is a harmless variety.

14. Find out in advance, if possible, the species of snakes prevalent in the area to which you are going, whether to vacation or to reside. Learn how to identify them and know their habits. A physician in the area can tell you whether you should obtain an anti-snake bite kit.

A hopeful final note to end this discussion—remember that most snakes are even more afraid of humans than humans are of snakes. If given an opportunity, they will scurry from a possible encounter as fast as they can.

LIZARD BITE

The only poisonous lizard in the United States is the Gila monster, which dwells in the desert country from southern Utah to northern Mexico, mainly inhabiting Arizona and New Mexico. This large, stout, sluggish lizard has granular scales and is colored pink or dull orange and black.

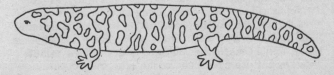

The venom of the Gila monster is considered more toxic than that of some poisonous snakes, and therefore, **immediate and proper first aid can be lifesaving.**

What to Do

1. Make the victim lie down at once.

2. **Keep the bitten part still** and in a position below the level of the heart. The victim should be kept dry and warm and not allowed to walk around. Any fear or excitement should be counteracted by reassurance that the victim will most probably be all right.

3. **Never give alcohol to the victim of a Gila monster bite.**

4. If the bite is on an extremity (feet, legs, hands, or arms), apply a constricting band or tourniquet (pp. 114-115) two to four inches closer to the heart than the site of the bite. If swelling progresses up the arm or leg, replace the constricting band or tourniquet closer to the heart than the swelling.

5. The constricting band or tourniquet should be tightened slightly. This will usually make the arm or leg bluish in color and make the veins stand out. It may also cause the bite to ooze. **It should not be so tight that the arm or leg is white.** If you know where the body pulses can be felt, check to see that a pulse is present below the constricting band or tourniquet.

6. Loosen the constricting band or tourniquet for a few seconds every fifteen minutes until the victim is under medical supervision.

7. Place an ice pack, if possible, directly over the bite, wherever the bite is located.

8. Call your doctor. If you are not near a telephone, carry the victim (pp. 41-48) to the nearest doctor or hospital for further treatment.

What NOT to Do

1. Do not let the victim walk.

2. Do not give him alcohol of any kind.

3. Do not use any narrow material such as rope, twine, or wire for the constricting band or tourniquet.

4. **Do not conceal the constricting band or tourniquet** —in this way you and others are reminded that it is there and needs to be loosened every fifteen minutes.

5. Do not use so-called "snake bite" remedies.

BLACK WIDOW SPIDER BITE

Spider bites from certain species may cause severe toxic symptoms. The most serious offender in the United States is the half-inch-long black widow spider. Instances of poisoning from its bite have been reported in almost every state, the fatality rate being over 5 per cent. The spider is shiny black with a reddish hourglass-shaped mark on the abdomen.

The tarantula—a large, sluggish, hairy spider—while also greatly feared and capable of a sharp bite, is *not* significantly poisonous to man.

Symptoms of Black Widow Spider Bite

The first symptom is usually a sharp, needlelike sting. Sometimes, however, the bite is not even felt at first. A burning sensation or a dull aching pain which spreads out and increases in severity may follow. Generalized muscle cramps may develop thirty to sixty minutes after the bite.

What to Do

1. Make the victim lie down at once.
2. **Keep the bitten part still** and in a position below the level of the heart. The victim should be kept dry and warm and not allowed to walk around. Any fear or excitement should be counteracted by reassurance that the victim will most probably be all right.
3. **Never give alcohol to the victim of a black widow spider bite.**
4. If the bite is on an extremity (feet, legs, hands, or arms), apply a constricting band or tourniquet (pp. 114-115) two to four inches closer to the heart than the site of the bite.
5. The constricting band or tourniquet should be tightened slightly. This will usually make the arm or

leg bluish in color and make the veins stand out. It may also cause the bite to ooze. **It should not be so tight that the arm or leg is white.** If you know where the body pulses can be felt, check to see that a pulse is present below the constricting band or tourniquet.

6. Loosen the constricting band or tourniquet for a few seconds every fifteen minutes until the victim is under medical supervision.

7. Place an ice pack, if possible, directly over the bite, wherever the bite is located.

8. Call your doctor. If you are not near a telephone, carry the victim (pp. 41-48) to the nearest doctor or hospital for further treatment, which may include the administration of antivenom.

What NOT to Do

1. Do not let the victim walk.

2. Do not give him alcohol of any kind.

3. Do not use any narrow material such as rope, twine, or wire for the constricting band or tourniquet.

4. **Do not conceal the constricting band or tourniquet** —in this way you and others are reminded that it is there and needs to be loosened every fifteen minutes.

5. Do not use so-called "snake bite" or "spider bite" remedies.

Prevention

In recent years new and effective insecticide sprays have been developed which can kill spiders on contact. Even the spraying of the web during the spider's absence is sometimes enough to kill her subsequently. The web of the black widow is easily recognized by the coarse thread which is spun irregularly in every direction.

In addition, the eradication of the spiders around human dwellings can be aided by general cleanliness, light, and the painting of the walls of infrequently used buildings. Bottoms of outdoor privy seats should be sprayed with an insecticide every three months. Rubbish and wood piles should not be moved without wearing gloves and a heavy shirt buttoned at the wrists.

SCORPION BITE

The stings of several varieties of scorpions in the Southwest are dangerously poisonous, especially to very young children. Adults almost always recover from scorpion bite. The severity of symptoms depends upon the size, and therefore, the age of the victim.

Some species of scorpions reach a length of four, five, or even eight inches. The stinger is always found at the tip of the curled tail.

What to Do
and What NOT to Do

Same as for Black Widow Spider Bite, pp. 121-122.

Prevention

The space under houses and boardwalks should be tightly enclosed and sprayed regularly with an insecticide. Rubbish should not be allowed to accumulate in any area where children play.

DOG BITE

Dogs appeared on the earth several million years before man, and it is certain that they have been biting man ever since their first prehistoric encounter. While dogs can bite for many reasons—for example, in play or because of their training to be watchdogs and protectors—some bites result because the animal is sick. The seriousness of the bite depends upon its location, its depth, and most importantly, whether the animal is suspected of having rabies.

A rabid dog can transmit the dread disease to humans

even by licking a scratch or the tiniest open place on the skin. While over five thousand dogs are reported to develop rabies annually in the United States, an average of only ten cases in humans occur per year. The disease is, unfortunately, always fatal.

Other animals which can transmit rabies to man by biting include cats, cattle, horses, sheep, and pigs— as well as bats, wolves, foxes, squirrels, coyotes, badgers, skunks, bears, and wildcats. Call your doctor immediately if you have been bitten by any of these animals.

What to Do

1. Wash the wound thoroughly with soap and water (tincture of green soap is very effective) to remove the saliva and disinfect the wound.

2. Rinse it with running water and apply a sterile dressing of gauze or an adhesive bandage strip.

3. Call your doctor at once, as further treatment may be necessary, as well as a program of immunization against rabies or tetanus.

The doctor may want to have the dog caught and observed. It is important not to kill the animal, unless it is threatening other people. If you must kill it, do not shoot or otherwise damage the dog in the head, because medical examination of the brain is the only certain way of establishing the diagnosis of rabies in a dead animal.

The doctor will also want to know whether the dog belongs to you and has been inoculated against rabies or whether the dog is an unknown animal. Also, describe the general behavior of the dog and the events leading up to and following the attack.

Inoculation against rabies should be given to all dogs and cats.

CAT BITE

Contrary to popular belief, cat bites are frequently more serious than those inflicted by dogs, because bacteria present in cats' mouths are more harmful to humans. In addition, cats can also carry rabies. Like a rabid dog, a rabid cat can transmit the dread disease to humans even by licking a scratch or the tiniest open place on the skin.

Other animals which can transmit rabies to man by

biting include dogs, cattle, horses, sheep, and pigs—as well as bats, wolves, foxes, squirrels, coyotes, badgers, skunks, bears, and wildcats. Call your doctor immediately if you have been bitten by any of these animals.

What to Do

1. Wash the area surrounding the bite with soap and water (tincture of green soap is very effective).
2. Apply a sterile dressing of gauze or an adhesive bandage strip.
3. Report the bite to your doctor at once, as further treatment may be necessary, as well as a program of immunization against rabies or tetanus.

The doctor may want to have the cat caught and observed. It is important not to kill it. The doctor will want to know whether the cat belongs to you and has been inoculated against rabies or whether it is a stray or unknown animal.

Inoculation against rabies should be given to all cats and dogs.

HUMAN BITES

Many people are unaware that human bites are potentially dangerous. Germs present in the mouth can cause severe infections through a break in the skin, tongue, or lips. Therefore, it is important to treat human bites promptly.

What to Do

1. Wash the wound immediately with soap and water (tincture of green soap is very effective).
2. Apply a sterile dressing of gauze or an adhesive bandage strip.
3. Call your doctor right away so he can decide on further treatment.

TICK BITES

The wood tick and the eastern dog tick can transmit Rocky Mountain spotted fever, a disease which occurs in the eastern part of the United States as well as in the West. In addition, certain ticks can cause a profound muscular weakness known as "tick paralysis" which can be fatal, especially in children. Others can cause a recurring fever known as "tick fever." Certain varieties of encephalitis (sleeping sickness) can also be transmitted by tick bites.

Ticks are flat, usually brown, about one fourth of an inch in length, and have eight legs. They adhere tenaciously to the skin or scalp, and it is important to remove them as quickly as possible to lessen the chance of disease.

What to Do

1. Apply oil (mineral, salad, or machine) to the body of the tick, which will interfere with its breathing. This will enable you to remove it completely without leaving its head imbedded in the skin.

2. The tick may come off right away. If not, let the oil remain in place for half an hour. Then remove the tick carefully with tweezers, taking time so all parts of the tick come away.

3. Scrub the area gently with soap and water because disease germs may be present on the skin.

4. Do **not** dig ticks out with tweezers or try to burn them out with lighted cigarettes—or try to remove them with your fingers.

5. Unless you can positively identify the tick as harmless, save it to show your doctor or local health authorities.

PORTUGUESE MAN-OF-WAR STINGS

A poisonous relative of the jellyfish, the Portuguese man-of-war is capable of inflicting injury to man ranging in severity from painful welts to shock and occasional death. Sometimes called the blue bottle, this brilliantly colored creature of the sea is not actually one animal, but a highly organized colony of dozens to hundreds of animals that function as one. It is generally found along the Eastern seaboard and in tropical waters.

When alive, the bladderlike blue body floats on the surface of the sea. Its numerous poisonous tentacles, which may exceed fifty feet in length, are concealed in the water. Even when washed up on the beach, the presumably dead Portuguese man-of-war can sting if a person touches its tentacles, as individual poison cells remain active for months.

What to Do

1. Scrub off any clinging or embedded parts of the tentacle with cold salt water at once.

2. Treat the welts with rubbing alcohol to neutralize the poison.

3. Take a hot shower. Then keep the stung arm or leg submerged in hot water for thirty to sixty minutes for relief of pain.

4. If pain is still present, take aspirin or any other pain reliever previously prescribed for you.

5. If pain still persists or is severe, call a doctor.

STINGRAY AND OTHER VENOMOUS FISH STINGS

Stingrays, though not common in North American waters, probably cause more injuries from direct contact than other venomous fish. These stings usually occur when the unwary victim steps on the animal while wading in the ocean surf or mud flats of a bay. For this reason, it is safer to use a shuffling gait rather than a stepping one while walking through sand or mud suspected of containing stingrays.

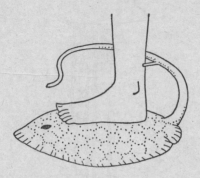

The barb or stinger in the stingray's tail is located near the **base** of the tail and usually breaks off in the wound, producing a very painful swelling. Its poison can also cause nausea, vomiting, abdominal pain, generalized muscular cramps, and moderate to marked weakness.

What to Do

1. Irrigate the wound immediately and thoroughly with the cold salt water at hand.

2. Remove the barb, if possible.

3. Soak the involved extremity (feet, legs, hands, arms) for thirty to sixty minutes in water as hot as the victim can tolerate it.

4. Then apply a sterile dressing.

5. Take the victim to a doctor or hospital in the event that further treatment is necessary.

Other marine creatures with venomous stings that are found in American waters include scorpion fish, bullhead or horned sharks, spiny dogfish, ratfish, sea urchins, and moray eels. The zebra fish, a relative of the scorpion fish, is found in the waters off Hawaii.

The treatment of stings from any of these venomous fish is the same as for stingray wounds.

Part Three

ILLNESSES

_____

— 19 —

CHEST PAIN

To many people any pain in the chest signifies heart
trouble or a heart attack, and brings accompanying
anxiety and dread. In actual fact, however, a heart
attack is only one of many causes of chest pain. So
if you develop chest pain, the first thing to remember
and to give you reassurance is that it is most probably
not originating from your heart—or from pneumonia or
pleurisy, two other common misconceptions.

HEART ATTACK SYMPTOMS

If chest pain is present (you must remember that
some heart attacks begin with symptoms of indigestion
rather than chest pain as in the case of former President
Eisenhower), it is usually located in the front of the
chest and most frequently in the center rather than
markedly on one side or the other.

The pain is usually described as a pressure or a
squeezing sensation which may be associated with pains
on one or both shoulders, or pains radiating into one
in both arms—even into the neck. It is usually not confused with "heartburn." (That is, it does not usually
have a burning quality.) Nausea, vomiting, a cold sweat,
and difficulty in breathing may be present. Usually one's
color turns pale.

Different Kinds of Pain

In general, any pain which is fleeting and comes in short twinges is **probably** not of any serious nature. But if a pain is extremely severe, you should, of course, call your doctor immediately. And if any pain or discomfort is continuously present for twenty to thirty minutes, you should call your doctor.

Sharp sticking pains (like the pains of the so-called "stitch"), which may be quite severe, usually do not signify heart trouble or other serious conditions.

What to Do

1. If you have a **persistent** or a **severe** pain in your chest, **call your doctor** and get into bed. If your stomach is not upset and if you do not feel nauseated, you should take either a jigger of whiskey, scotch, or brandy, or else a sedative such as a half grain of phenobarbital or one or two tablets of a tranquilizer, if available. If you feel you cannot keep anything in your stomach, it is best not to take anything by mouth.

2. Whether you are nauseated or not, ice-cold drinks should be avoided, although it is permissible to chew on chips of ice. You should then get into a comfortable position, either in a chair or in bed, and, if possible, try to divert your mind by talking, reading, or watching television.

3. It is important to avoid getting chilled; so if you have been out in cold weather or in a cold environment of any kind, get into a warmer atmosphere as quickly as possible. If you are in a very hot environment, especially if you are having any trouble getting your breath, it will be helpful to get good ventilation and into air conditioning, if possible.

4. If you feel faint or dizzy, it is better to lie down rather than sit up, even if that means lying down on the ground or floor, taking care not to be chilled. However, if you are short of breath, you will probably feel more comfortable sitting up.

5. *If you have had a heart attack in the past, or have been under medical care for a heart condition,* you should get specific instructions from your doctor about what to do in case you develop a pain in your chest. You should follow the same advice outlined in this

section—unless your doctor has given you other instructions (for example, he may have told you to take your nitroglycerin tablets or other medication in the event of certain kinds of chest pain).

LUNG PROBLEMS

Sudden sharp chest pains, often made worse by breathing, may make a deep breath impossible. They can "take your breath away" or make your breathing "catch." Such pains may arise from the common "stitch" (often experienced upon exertion), from strained chest wall muscles, from a bruised or broken rib, or very rarely from a sudden collapse of the lung (spontaneous pneumothorax).

Most people worry that chest pains signify pneumonia or pleurisy, but these conditions rarely come on suddenly. Both are usually preceded or accompanied by a cold or coughing, or some degree of fever.

What to Do

1. Call your doctor if sharp chest pains persist for twenty to thirty minutes, or if you have any trouble breathing at the end of this time.

2. Find a comfortable position and remain still. Lying on the affected side will splint (or immobilize) it, frequently relieving pain.

3. Avoid taking deep breaths and avoid coughing, if possible.

4. A jigger of whiskey, scotch, or brandy will offer some relief. In addition, one can safely take two aspirin tablets or a half-grain codeine tablet.

5. Take and record your temperature and pulse (pp. 35-36).

20

INTERNAL BLEEDING

The sight of blood and its brilliant red color has been known to make brave men faint and onlookers panic. While one need not faint or panic, it is a good thing that we are alarmed when we see blood. In fact, bleeding is one of nature's warnings to which we react instinctively.

However, it is also well to remember that the average adult, having five to six quarts of blood in his circulation, can, if his health is otherwise good, tolerate the rapid loss of one pint of blood and the slower loss of even larger quantities without harm. It takes less than one tenth of a pint of blood to completely stain a handkerchief, to color the urine red, or to redden a toilet bowl.

NOSEBLEEDS

The vast majority of nosebleeds can be stopped in the home with simple measures. The best position is to sit up with the head bent slightly forward—**not** lying down or with the head bent lower than the level of the heart.

Take two small pieces of cotton and saturate them with ordinary household (3 per cent) hydrogen peroxide (cold water will do if peroxide is not available). Squeeze out the excess fluid and insert the moistened cotton into the lower three quarters of an inch of each nostril.

Once these are inserted, exert pressure with thumb and index finger on either side of the lowest part of the nose, thereby compressing the nostrils.

Do not talk, eat, chew, drink, or further manipulate the nose. If the cotton becomes so saturated with blood that there is leakage, remove it and insert a freshly moistened piece. Changing of cotton should be kept to a minimum. Usually the bleeding will subside within fifteen minutes to half an hour. It may also be helpful to apply an ice bag to the back of the neck. If some blood accumulates in the back of the throat, it can be expectorated or even swallowed without harm.

Once the bleeding has stopped for at least fifteen minutes, remoisten the cotton which is in the nose by means of a dropper. Remove the cotton very delicately and slowly. It is extremely important not to blow, rub the nose, sneeze, or pick at the encrusted blood, as any of these activities may start the bleeding anew. Call your doctor if bleeding persists or occurs often.

BLEEDING FROM THE MOUTH

Bleeding from the lips, tongue, gums, or inner cheek is treated by direct pressure on the bleeding area. The commonest causes are falls (in children), blows, cuts from accidental biting of the lips or tongue or those resulting from a convulsion.

There is no need to worry about swallowing small amounts of blood, but if possible, try to avoid swallowing large amounts of blood, which may result in nausea and vomiting.

What to Do

1. Locate the source of bleeding and apply direct pressure to the cut or torn area, preferably using sterile gauze or a clean cloth.

2. Maintain the pressure continuously until the bleeding stops.

3. Call your physician (or dentist if the bleeding comes from an extraction or oral surgery, p. 203).

4. Sucking on an ice cube (or, for children, a popsicle) will relieve pain and help to stop the bleeding.

BLEEDING FROM THE EAR

Bleeding from the **outside** of the ear should be treated by direct pressure applied to the bleeding site with sterile gauze or the cleanest cloth available. The pressure should be maintained until the bleeding stops.

Bleeding from **within** the ear may be serious—not because of blood loss, but because it may indicate a skull fracture. On the other hand, something as minor as a scratch in the ear canal can cause bleeding from this area. In either case, because of the danger of infection, do **not** put anything into the ear and do **not** irrigate it.

Any bleeding from the inside of the ear should be reported to your doctor without delay.

VAGINAL BLEEDING

Every woman who has experienced menstruation can distinguish her normal flow from heavier or more profuse bleeding. Should excessive bleeding occur, get into bed and remain there, after preparing an ice bag to apply to the lower abdomen while resting.

Call your doctor. Keep track of how many tampons or napkins are used. Also note whether the color of the blood is bright or dark, and whether there are clots. All this information may prove helpful to the doctor.

RECTAL BLEEDING

Most people are alarmed when they see that blood has come from the rectal area. Blood noted only on the toilet paper, and not in the toilet bowl, is in all probability coming from the surface, usually from a minor abrasion of the skin or a small crack (fissure). This is not a dangerous condition, but should be reported to your doctor, who may want to examine you. The same applies to streaks of blood seen on the surface of a bowel movement.

The passage of pure blood from the rectum is a potential emergency. You should get into bed with an ice bag on the lower abdomen and remain quiet. **Call your doctor.** The number of bowel movements or passages of blood is important information for the doctor and should be recorded.

Bloody diarrhea should be reported to your doctor right away.

The passage of **a black bowel movement**—the so-called "tarry" stool—should be considered as being due to bleeding higher up in the intestinal tract, unless one is taking iron or other medication known to color the stools black. A black bowel movement should lead one to **call the doctor without delay,** and to remain in bed until he arrives.

VOMITING OF BLOOD

The vomiting of blood may not be clearly recognized because the stomach acid causes blood to turn brown, giving it the appearance of coffee or coffee grounds. Whether the vomitus is dark brown or red, this signifies a potential emergency and **your doctor should be notified at once.** Get into bed and remain quiet. Nothing should be taken by mouth, but you can chew on ice if you are thirsty.

COUGHING UP OF BLOOD

One should distinguish between the appearance of pinkish or blood-streaked sputum, which is not dangerous, and the coughing up of pure blood, which can be serious. In the former, while the blood loss is not harmful in itself, the symptom must be called to the doctor's attention, as any amount of blood in the sputum is not normal.

In the event that the material coughed up is **pure blood, call your doctor right away,** get into bed, and remain as quiet as possible until he comes.

21

STOMACH, INTESTINAL, AND RECTAL DISORDERS

ABDOMINAL PAIN, NAUSEA, AND VOMITING

Abdominal pain, nausea, and vomiting can occur separately or together. They can be produced by a great variety of conditions—ranging from simple indigestion or "upset stomach" to intestinal flu, food poisoning, irritable colon, female disorders, stomach ulcers, gall bladder attacks, and appendicitis.

To discover the cause of abdominal pain, nausea, and vomiting may require all the diagnostic skill of the well-trained physician, so *do not be your own diagnostician.* **If pain, nausea, or vomiting persists or recurs or is without obvious explanation, call your doctor.** From your description alone, he may be able to reassure you. If he feels he needs to see you, he may tell you what to do until he examines you.

In the presence of abdominal pain, nausea, or vomiting:

1. Do not take or give a cathartic or laxative unless specifically ordered by your doctor.

2. Do not take or give anything by mouth (this includes food, water, alcohol, liquids, and medicine) unless specifically ordered by your doctor.

3. Take and record your temperature and pulse (pp. 35-36), as this may help your doctor to make a diagnosis,

4. Get into bed and apply an electric heating pad or hot water bottle to the painful area, being careful not to burn your abdomen.

Appendicitis is an inflammation of the appendix—a hollow, wormlike structure attached to one end of the large intestine and usually located on the right side of the abdomen below the level of the waist. The treatment of appendicitis is surgical removal, because an inflamed appendix may rupture and cause peritonitis. While appendicitis occurs more frequently in younger people, it can occur at any age.

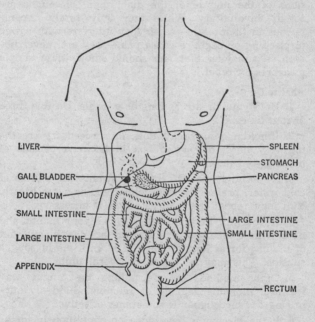

Gall bladder attacks occur when stones in the gall bladder, or in the ducts leading from the gall bladder to the intestine, cause severe spasms. Gallstones may also result in acute inflammation of the gall bladder itself. The pain of an acute gall bladder attack is often severe, usually located in the upper right side of the abdomen. It may spread to the right shoulder blade or shoulder, or go straight through to the back.

Stomach ulcers are erosions in the lining of the stomach (gastric ulcer) or the duodenum (duodenal ulcer). The duodenum connects the outlet of the stomach with the beginning of the small intestine. Heartburn or a boring pain in the stomach area which occurs more frequently than once a week could be the first symptom of a stomach ulcer.

PROTRACTED HICCOUGHS

Hiccoughs have been known throughout the history of man. They occur in the unborn child and in people of all ages. Nothing more or less than periodic contractions of the muscle of the diaphragm, hiccoughs are totally involuntary. While they only rarely become serious in themselves—when they interfere with eating or sleeping or begin to cause pain—they are, nevertheless, so annoying that one should know these simple measures for relief.

What to Do

1. Hold your breath as long as possible. Do this three or four times.

2. If holding your breath does not succeed, try breathing very hard, deep, and fast in between periods of holding your breath.

3. If hiccoughs persist, then try swallowing a glass of cold water, preferably iced, while holding your breath. You may repeat this at least once, if necessary.

4. If you still have no relief, cover your mouth and nose with a small paper bag and breathe in and out of the bag for as long as you can or until the hiccoughs subside. This may be repeated several times.

5. Other methods include pulling the tongue way forward, inducing gagging or retching. Suddenly surprising the hiccougher is sometimes effective.

6. If the hiccoughs have gone on continuously for as long as half an hour without response to these measures, call your doctor, as he may want to advise you to take certain medications or to give you an injection.

DIARRHEA

Diarrhea, the unusually frequent passage of soft or liquid bowel movements, can be a symptom of a variety of infectious, toxic, or functional disorders. Persistent or recurrent diarrhea should not be ignored. You should also note if there is any blood in the stool, as this is a sign which should be reported to your doctor without delay.

The commonest causes of diarrhea of short duration are laxative foods (such as bran, figs, prunes), spoiled food, and virus infections. If diarrhea occurs without pain, vomiting, or fever, and if no blood is seen in the stool, follow this advice:

What to Do

1. Take nothing by mouth for up to twelve hours.

2. If you are thirsty, you may chew on ice cubes or crushed ice. Later on, you may take sips of water, weak tea, ginger ale, or clear broth, and repeat at frequent intervals. You may need to stay on these clear liquids for twenty-four to forty-eight hours.

3. Lying in bed with an electric heating pad or a hot water bottle applied to the abdomen may be helpful. Be careful not to burn your abdomen.

4. Once the diarrhea has been brought under control, very gradually begin to eat such bland foods as salt crackers, dry or melba toast, flavored gelatin desserts, mashed or baked potato, white rice, cooked or dry rice cereals, or jellied consommé. Later you may add a soft-boiled or poached egg, cooked carrots or peas, a thin slice of white meat chicken or turkey.

If you get any recurrence of diarrhea, loss of appetite, or nausea after introducing any of these solid foods, again omit food and liquids for four to six hours, and then gradually return to clear liquids and the foods listed above.

5. Avoid any raw fruits or vegetables, coffee, spices (other than salt), and rich, fatty, or fried foods.

6. While anti-diarrhea remedies containing kaolin, pectin, bismuth, certain antibiotics, and other ingredients may be sold without prescription, it is generally advisable to consult your doctor before taking any medication.

HARD STOOL IN THE RECTUM

Occasionally fecal matter in the rectum becomes so hard that it is impossible to eliminate it. This is called fecal impaction. It can be caused by certain medications or the taking of barium (either by mouth or by rectum) for X-ray studies. It tends to occur more frequently in the elderly, the bedridden, and occasionally, at any age, after long automobile or train rides.

There is a sense of fullness in the rectum, and often marked rectal pain during unsuccessful attempts at evacuation. In the elderly and bedridden, fecal impaction may be a cause of intestinal blockage, distension, fever, and, paradoxically, diarrhea.

Fecal impaction is the most acute and painful form of constipation. Ordinary constipation tends to persist over days, weeks, or years, whereas fecal impaction occurs infrequently, sometimes only once and never again.

What to Do

1. Insert one or more plain glycerin rectal suppositories. This may help lubricate the rectum and soften the fecal matter. Or you may use one of the over-the-counter suppositories (frequently advertised for hemorrhoids) which contain not only a lubricant, but a local anesthetic as well.

2. If the above is unsuccessful, warm three ounces of mineral or olive oil to bath temperature and use as an enema, retaining it as long as possible in order to soften fecal matter before expelling. This can be repeated, if necessary.

3. If you are still unsuccessful, using a rubber finger cot or condom well lubricated with petroleum jelly, insert a finger into the rectum. Attempt to break up the impaction into smaller pieces which can be removed by the finger or evacuated.

4. If the above methods of relieving fecal impaction have not helped you, call your doctor.

5. Even if you are successful in relieving the impaction by yourself, report its occurrence to your doctor.

HEMORRHOIDS (PILES) AND ANAL FISSURES

Extremely common in adults of both sexes, hemorrhoids are actually dilated veins in the region of the anal opening. Like varicose veins in the leg, they are the result of the pull of gravity on vertical man.

Hemorrhoids may bulge or protrude, causing little or no pain, except in the case of **prolapsed** hemorrhoids—

a condition in which the rectal lining protrudes after a bowel movement and may fail to return spontaneously. Hemorrhoids may bleed and may become clotted (thrombosed). This last condition can be severely painful, especially during the passage of a bowel movement and even when sitting down. It usually appears suddenly with a local area of slight to moderate swelling, hardness, and marked tenderness to the touch.

Anal fissures are small cracks or breaks in the lining around the opening. They, too, can be very painful, particularly during defecation.

Whether painful or not, report any suspected hemorrhoids or abnormal rectal condition to your doctor.

What to Do

1. Take sitz baths (sitting in a bathtub filled with four to five inches of water as hot as you can stand it) from four to six times a day. This generally brings relief, but, if it does not, lie down in bed on your side and apply an ice bag to the affected area.

2. Call your doctor for further advice.

– 22 –

HERNIA (RUPTURE)

The occurrence of a hernia or "rupture" is rarely a sudden event. Even when it is, there is usually no cause for immediate action. A protrusion of intestinal lining or a loop of intestine through a weakened part of the abdominal wall, a hernia is found most frequently in three places—in the groin, at the umbilicus (navel), or through an abdominal surgical incision when the scar has weakened.

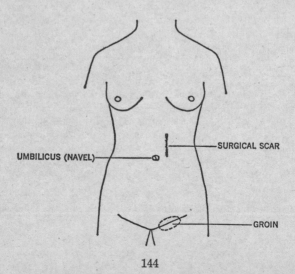

When It Is Serious

Some hernias do not require any treatment whatsoever; there have been individual cases in which hernias have been present for years and even decades without causing the patient any trouble. Other hernias can cause sufficient pain and disability to make an operation necessary at a future date.

However, a hernia which rapidly becomes painful or swollen or cannot be reduced—that is, pushed back into the abdominal cavity—may indicate a real emergency. This most frequently happens in the case of hernias in the groin, which are called femoral or inguinal hernias.

The immediate danger is that the hernia may become strangulated, causing so much tissue damage that the condition may lead to blockage of the intestine. Strangulation may also impair the blood supply to the intestine, causing inflammation and possible gangrene.

What to Do

1. If a hernia becomes painful, begins to swell, or seems impossible to reduce (push back in), prepare an ice bag (see next paragraph) and go right to bed. Lie down flat on your back or, preferably, with the bottom of the bed elevated. (Have someone else place books or blocks under the foot of the bed—the patient should remain quiet.) This will take the pressure off the hernia and may allow for reduction by means of **gentle** manipulation of the hernia and its contents.

2. If the hernia is not successfully reduced within fifteen or twenty minutes, then apply the ice bag to the hernia, which will decrease the tenderness as well as the size. After another half hour you should repeat the manipulation. If this attempt proves unsuccessful, then call the doctor, keeping the ice bag in place until he arrives or gives specific instructions.

3. In any case, report to your doctor any suspected hernia and any persistent or recurrent pain in the groin.

— 23 —

KIDNEY AND BLADDER

EMERGENCIES

The kidneys, the bladder, the ureters (long, thin tubes connecting the kidneys to the bladder), and the urethra (the urinary channel from the bladder to the exterior) comprise what doctors refer to as the genitourinary tract. In men the prostate gland, penis, scrotum, and testicles are included—in women the ovaries, uterus (or womb), Fallopian tubes, and vagina. (See illustrations.)

Fortunately, there are few true emergencies of the genitourinary tract. However, prompt recognition and proper early treatment in those emergencies which do occur can help to make the patient more comfortable, can prevent some serious consequences, and can hasten complete recovery.

INJURIES

Since the kidneys are deeply situated and protected by heavy back muscles and the lower rib cage, injury to them is rare—unless the force or trauma has been

146

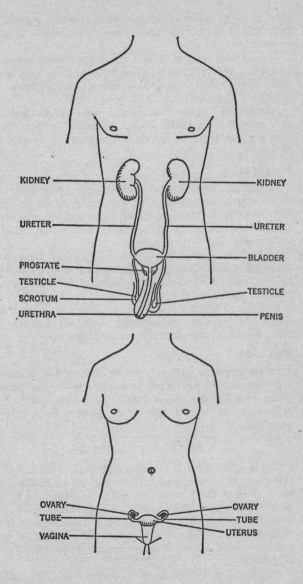

severe, as in automobile accidents, contact sports, or bad falls. Injury may also occur from bullet or stab wounds.

The bladder is most commonly injured when a person sustains a pelvic fracture. Blast injuries from explosions and bullet or stab wounds may also tear or perforate the bladder.

Injuries of the scrotum, penis, urethra, or testicles may result from kicks, blows, wounds, or falls. It is rare for the female reproductive system to sustain an injury.

Signs of Injury

The most important and obvious sign of kidney injury is the appearance of blood in the urine, although there can be internal bleeding around the kidney with pain and tenderness in the kidney area (above the waist on either side of the backbone).

In bladder injury there may be internal leakage of urine from the bladder, producing pain and tenderness in the lower abdomen, often inability to urinate, and possibly blood in the urine.

Injuries to the male urethra, penis, scrotum, and testicles are usually immediately apparent because of pain, swelling, discoloration, or tenderness.

What to Do

In all suspected injuries of the genitourinary system **a doctor should be called immediately—or the patient taken to a hospital immediately.** Keep him lying down and warm in transit. Give him as smooth a ride as possible.

INABILITY TO URINATE

The sudden onset of inability to urinate, acute urinary retention, is an extremely distressing and painful experience. Unless there has been injury as described in the previous section, retention tends to occur most frequently in older men, and is most commonly due to enlargement of the prostate gland. There may or may not have been warning symptoms or prior difficulty in urinating.

Aggravating factors may be spicy foods or alcohol, certain medications, exposure to cold, attempts to hold the urine back for too long a time, long automobile or train rides, infections, the passage of blood clots or a bladder stone, sexual excesses, and enforced bed rest.

What to Do

1. Have the person get into a warm bath and encourage him to void while still in the tub—or apply warm, moist packs to the lower abdomen and genital area. If either method will work, it should do so within an hour.

2. Call your physician if you are unsuccessful.

3. Even if the person finally has been able to urinate, an episode of this kind should be reported to a physician.

SEVERE KIDNEY PAIN IN THE BACK

This pain, which usually is located in the kidney area —above the waist on either side of the backbone—may travel down the side of the abdomen and into the groin or genital area (scrotum and penis in men, vagina in women). It can be one of the most excruciating pains known to man, and is usually caused by a stone in the kidney or ureter.

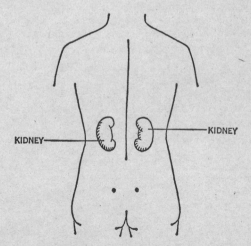

It may be associated with nausea and vomiting, the frequent desire to urinate, burning on urination, and occasionally passage of blood in the urine.

What to Do

1. Call your doctor.

2. Have the patient get into a hot bath and remain until some relief is obtained. After he gets out of the tub, apply hot moist packs, a hot water bottle or electric heating pad to the painful area.

3. **Save all urine** in a clean glass container, as the doctor will want to examine it.

— 24 —

DIABETIC EMERGENCIES

While the 1,600,000 known diabetics in the United States are almost always taught how to take care of themselves and how to deal with potentially serious problems, the non-diabetic members of a household may be less familiar with what to do when certain emergency situations arise. It is especially for them that this chapter is written.

There are an additional estimated 1,400,000 diabetics in this country who do not know they have the disease. Hundreds of thousands more—prediabetics—may develop it. It is important for older persons and anyone with a family history of diabetes to eat a balanced diet, avoid overweight, and have periodic physical examinations.

DIABETIC ACIDOSIS

Acidosis is a disturbance of the body chemistry in which there is **too little insulin** for the body's requirements. The blood sugar is too high, there is a large amount of **sugar in the urine,** and the diabetes is out of control.

The patient may complain of:
Weakness
Drowsiness
Excessive thirst
Increased urination
Loss of appetite (possibly followed by nausea and
vomiting)
Abdominal pain
Other signs:
Skin dry and usually flushed
Breathing deep and rapid
Acetone odor (a sweetish smell) to the breath
Fever
Pulse weak and rapid
Excessive sleepiness which can progress to a state
of coma

What to Do

If a known diabetic develops the symptoms or signs
just listed, suspect diabetic acidosis.

1. Call your doctor right away.

2. Keep the patient quiet, warm, and as comfortable
as possible until the doctor arrives.

3. Take and record the person's temperature and
pulse (pp. 35-36).

4. If possible, save a specimen of urine for the doctor,
as he may want to test it for sugar and acetone.

5. If possible, try to find out whether the person is
taking insulin or any other medication. If he is taking
insulin, find out what kind of insulin, how many units,
and when the last dose was taken.

6. If the patient vomits, try to save some of the
vomitus, as the doctor may want to examine it.

7. Do not give alcohol in any form.

8. Do not give any medication unless the doctor orders
it.

9. If the patient is thirsty, and is not nauseated or
vomiting, offer him fruit juice, salty broth or bouillon,
tea or water.

INSULIN (OR LOW BLOOD SUGAR) REACTION

Insulin reaction occurs when the blood sugar level is excessively lowered by **too much insulin** or anti-diabetic pills or too little food.

The patient may complain of:

Hunger

Sweating

Nervousness

Jitteriness

Weakness which may be of sudden onset

Dizziness

Headache

Double vision

Palpitations

Other signs:

Skin moist and pale

Breathing normal or shallow

Pulse full and strong

Confusion and/or strange behavior which can progress to unconsciousness

Muscular twitching

Convulsions

In contrast to diabetic acidosis, there is **no** excessive thirst, deep breathing, increased urination, or abdominal pain—vomiting and acetone odor to the breath very rarely occur.

What to Do

If a known diabetic who is taking insulin (or pills to control his diabetes) develops the symptoms or signs just listed, suspect insulin (or low blood sugar) reaction and . . .

1. Immediately give the patient one of the following: sugar, candy, syrup, honey, jam, jelly, fruit juice—or a bottled or canned soft drink containing sugar. If none of these is available, give fresh or canned fruit, cookies, bread, or cake.

2. Then give the person milk, any milk drink, ice cream, custard, or a gelatin dessert.

3. Call your doctor.

4. Keep the patient as quiet and comfortable as possible until the doctor arrives.

5. If the patient is taking insulin, try to find out what kind of insulin, how many units, and when the last dose was taken. If he is taking pills for his diabetes, try to find out what kind of pills they are, how many were taken today, and when they were last taken.

6. Do not give alcohol or any medication unless the doctor orders it.

7. Some diabetics, especially children and adolescents, are prone to recurrent insulin reactions. Your family doctor should be informed if a member of your household experiences repeated insulin reactions, as he may then want to instruct you in the use of a new and safe emergency treatment using an injection of glucagon.

— 25 —

PHLEBITIS

Phlebitis is an inflammation of the veins, most commonly occurring in the legs. Blood clots may form in the veins, sometimes with serious consequences. It is for this reason that early recognition and treatment as well as methods of prevention are important.

Any of the symptoms listed below should raise the suspicion of phlebitis. However, the same symptoms may be due to a variety of more common and less potentially serious conditions. Only your doctor can decide after talking with you and possibly examining you.

When to Suspect Phlebitis

1. If you have any persistent pain or discomfort in the calf or inner thigh area or in a varicose vein, especially if accompanied by tenderness upon pressure.

2. If you have any unusual warmth or redness in any of these areas.

3. If you develop any swelling or a feeling of fullness or heaviness in one leg.

If you suspect phlebitis, call your doctor without delay. Get into bed, lie flat, and elevate the affected leg with pillows.

Factors in Susceptibility

Injury to the legs and infections below the knee can lead to phlebitis. Phlebitis without injury or infection rarely occurs in children or adolescents. It tends to occur most frequently after operations and childbirth, during pregnancy, in the course of prolonged bed rest, in people who are overweight, and in those with bad varicose veins.

Prevention

1. During long motor trips, train rides, and airplane flights, arrange to get up and walk around for five minutes at least every hour.

2. Avoid wearing garters and pantie girdles that are too tight around the thighs.

3. Avoid sitting with your legs crossed.

— 26 —

CANCER WARNINGS

The American Cancer Society estimates that every year nearly a hundred thousand Americans needlessly die of cancer, mainly because their disease was not recognized in time. A great number were either too ignorant —or too scared—to avail themselves of medical help.

Much publicity has been given to danger signals of cancer—there are some who say that people have been made **too** cancer-conscious. Because the chances for complete cure or effective control are better now than they have ever been, **it is more important than ever to know** what symptoms or signs can be the earliest indications of cancer.

Sometimes merely a telephone call to your doctor can bring prompt and secure reassurance that your symptoms are *not* due to cancer. At other times your doctor will want to examine you or make certain tests. For those who have no symptoms, a periodic physical examination is the best—and usually the only—way of detecting cancer in its earliest stages.

The following is a list of symptoms or signs which should impel you to call your doctor:

1. Any persistent lump or nodule on or under the skin—any unexplained swelling of a bone or joint.

2. Any wart or mole that changes in size or color.

3. Any sore on the skin, in the mouth, or on the lips or tongue which fails to heal.

4. Any lump in the breast or discharge from the nipple, especially if bloody.

5. Any unaccountable change in bowel or bladder habits.

6. The passage of black or tarry stools or blood by rectum.

7. Any persistent unexplained cough, especially if associated with shortness of breath, wheezing, or blood-tinged sputum.

8. Progressive or persistent hoarseness.

9. Any persistent difficulty in swallowing.

10. Any persistent or unexplained indigestion or loss of appetite.

11. Any persistently swollen glands in the neck, armpits, or groin.

12. Any menstrual bleeding or bloody vaginal discharge occurring after the menopause or outside of a regular menstrual period (including bleeding following sexual relations or douching).

13. The appearance of blood in the urine.

14. A bloody nasal discharge.

15. Progressive or unexplained headaches.

16. Unexplained weight loss.

17. Unexplained fever lasting two weeks or longer.

18. Any persistent, unexplained pain.

Part Four

HEAD AND BRAIN INJURIES AND DISORDERS

— 27 —

HEAD INJURIES

The human skull is so designed that from infancy to old age the brain is amazingly well protected. However, the results of injuries to the head may range from a simple headache to a concussion—which literally means a shaking of the brain and is associated with temporary unconsciousness.

More serious injuries can be responsible for skull fractures and varying degrees of temporary or permanent brain damage. The victim is dazed or unconscious, and therefore cannot give an account of how he was injured—nor may he even be aware of other (possibly more severe) injuries such as a broken neck or broken back. If there is blood or clear, watery fluid—even in small amounts—coming from the nose or ear after a head injury, a skull fracture should be suspected.

What to Do
if the Victim Is Conscious or Unconscious

1. Call a doctor **immediately.**

2. Place the victim flat on his back with his head raised slightly and turned to one side so that blood, vomitus, and/or other fluids can flow easily from the mouth—and so that his tongue will stay forward and leave the air passage free.

3. Loosen any tight clothing around the neck.

4. Keep the victim comfortably warm.

161

5. Do not move him from this position until medical help arrives on the scene unless absolutely necessary, as in case of fire (pp. 41-48).

6. Do not give anything by mouth.

7. If the victim is unconscious and his breathing is extremely labored or noisy, begin mouth-to-mouth breathing (pp. 23-29) and continue until breathing is spontaneous and unlabored—or until medical assistance arrives.

8. If there is heavy bleeding or spurting of blood from a scalp or skin wound, apply pressure directly over the wound with as clean a dressing as possible—a clean handkerchief or part of a clean sheet or shirt. A sterile gauze pad is, of course, preferable, if available.

If there is nothing available to make a pressure dressing, close the wound with your hand or fingers, applying enough pressure to stop the bleeding.

What to Do
if the Victim Is a Child

If a baby or young child stops crying within fifteen minutes after the accident, maintains a good color, and does not vomit, he has probably **not** injured his brain.

However, **call your doctor without delay** if the child loses consciousness immediately or later.

The doctor should also be called:

1. If the child vomits or does not want to eat.

2. If he remains pale for several hours.

3. If he complains of headache or dizziness after an hour.

4. If he acts drowsy or seems dazed.

An open wound on the scalp or face may bleed profusely. Treat it as you would a wound anywhere else (pp. 68-69).

SEVERE OR UNUSUAL HEADACHE

Even though a bad headache in itself is no more of an emergency than pain elsewhere in the body, it is helpful to know how to minimize the discomfort until you can reach your doctor for advice.

The great majority of severe headaches are brought on by causes which are not serious. However, you should call your doctor 1) if there is no obvious explanation for the headache (such as tension, fever, eye strain, or hunger); 2) if the headache is dramatically sudden in its onset; 3) if you have never experienced a similar headache before; or 4) if the headache is not relieved by previously effective medications.

You should also consult your physician if you suffer from chronic or recurrent headaches.

What to Do
for a Severe or Unusual Headache

1. Take and record your temperature.

2. Call your doctor.

3. See that the room is cool and well ventilated.

4. Since strong lights may be irritating, pull down the shades or blinds during the day and keep the room dimly lit at night.

5. An ice bag wrapped in a face towel or a cold washcloth applied to the area of greatest pain will usually give some relief.

6. Lie down in the position which is most comfortable to you.

— 29 —

DIZZINESS AND VERTIGO

Dizziness is a feeling of unsteadiness centered in the head. It may be called fuzziness, lightheadedness, or giddiness, and can affect the equilibrium to such a degree that a person may have difficulty walking or standing. He may have the feeling he is going to fall or faint; he may weave or stagger.

Vertigo is a more extreme form of dizziness in which a person has the distinct sensation of spinning or turning—or that all surrounding objects are whirling or revolving about him. Severe forms of vertigo are associated with nausea and vomiting.

While both dizziness and vertigo can be extremely frightening and incapacitating, only a few of the many causes of these conditions are a serious threat to health.

What to Do

1. Have the person lie down.

2. Adjust the head to the elevation and position that is most comfortable and have him remain quiet. Keeping the eyes closed may give additional relief.

3. Call your doctor if dizziness persists or if there is vertigo, nausea, or vomiting.

— 30 —

FAINTING

Fainting is a sudden but brief loss of consciousness due to interference with the circulation to the brain. The most common form of loss of consciousness, fainting is frightening to witness. However, in the great majority of instances, it is not caused by serious illness.

Common causes of fainting include standing motionless for a long period of time, being overheated, receiving a sudden emotional shock, going without food for many hours, and getting out of bed suddenly, especially after having been bedridden because of illness.

What to Do

1. Place the person perfectly flat (without a pillow) where he has fainted.

2. Then lift his legs straight up in the air, which improves the circulation of blood to the brain. Hold his legs in this position until consciousness returns, which is generally only a matter of minutes.

3. Loosen any tight clothing around the neck.

4. If the room is stuffy, open the windows or turn on the air conditioning.

5. After the person has regained consciousness, allow him to lie on his back until he feels well enough to sit up.

6. Let him remain sitting for fifteen minutes. If he still feels well, then you can allow him to walk around.

7. If at any time he starts to feel faint again or to turn pale, have him lie down and elevate his legs once again.

8. Call a doctor if faintness persists while lying down or if fainting recurs while lying down—or if the person does not feel well enough to sit up or to walk around.

9. Any episode of fainting should be reported to your doctor.

Prevention

If a person feels faint, have him lie perfectly flat (without a pillow). Then have him lift his legs straight up in the air. Help him to hold them in this position until he feels back to normal.

If the person is unable or unwilling to lie down where he is, the next best thing is to have him sit with his knees spread wide apart and put his head far down between them. Take care to see that he does not topple forward.

If there is nothing to sit on, a person can prevent fainting by standing with the legs apart and bending forward at the waist so that his head is about at the level of his knees.

— 31 —

UNCONSCIOUSNESS

While fainting is a common, usually harmless, and brief form of unconsciousness, any state of unconsciousness lasting longer than five to ten minutes indicates a condition which demands immediate medical attention. It is also important to seek medical help for anyone who seems dazed, confused, cannot respond appropriately to questions or instructions, or seems to have a loss of memory.

Unconsciousness can be caused by anything which disturbs or impairs the function of the brain. Some common causes are: head injury or concussion, accidental or intentional poisoning or overdosage, asphyxiation (as from drowning or carbon monoxide), convulsions, severe heart attack, stroke, diabetic coma or insulin overdosage, excessive alcoholic intake, acute infections of the nervous system such as polio or meningitis, severe allergic reactions, heatstroke.

What to Do

1. Call a doctor **immediately.**

2. Place the victim flat on his back with his head turned to one side so that blood, vomitus, and/or other fluids can flow easily from the mouth, and so that his tongue will stay forward and leave the air passage free.

3. Loosen any tight clothing around the neck.

4. Keep the victim comfortably warm.

167

5. Do not move him from this position until medical help arrives on the scene unless absolutely necessary, as in the case of fire (pp. 41-48).

6. Do not give anything by mouth.

7. If his breathing stops or is extremely labored or noisy, begin mouth-to-mouth breathing (pp. 23-29) and continue until breathing is spontaneous and unlabored —or until medical assistance arrives.

8. If there is heavy bleeding or spurting of blood from a scalp or skin wound, apply pressure directly over the wound with as clean a dressing as possible— a clean handkerchief or part of a clean sheet or shirt. A sterile gauze pad is, of course, preferable, if available.

If there is nothing available to make a pressure dressing, close the wound with your hand or fingers, applying enough pressure to stop the bleeding.

9. Look for any medical identification the person may carry or wear. It will help the doctor to know **1)** if the victim is a known diabetic or epileptic; or **2)** if he is seriously allergic to certain medications; or **3)** if he is taking any medication to thin his blood (anticoagulants).

— 32 —

CONVULSIONS

Convulsions, also known as "fits," seizures, or epileptic attacks, were first described by Hippocrates about 400 B.C. They are a series of unnatural, involuntary, and often violent muscular contractions, usually affecting the entire body and associated with unconsciousness. They may be caused by high fever in children, by epilepsy, and by certain other disorders of the brain and the circulation to it.

Convulsions in themselves do not do any harm to the brain. While they are frightening to witness, convulsions are almost never a medical emergency and are rarely a cause for serious injury. Neither are they especially associated with mental deficiency or insanity.

Famous figures who suffered from convulsions include Julius Caesar, Alexander the Great, Napoleon, Mohammed, Beethoven, Schumann, Handel, Tchaikowsky, Dante, Dickens, Molière, Lord Byron, Tolstoy, Cardinal Richelieu, Van Gogh, Isaac Newton, and Alfred Nobel (Nobel Prize).

What to Do

1. Place the subject on a rug or bed, if possible, and **keep him on his side** rather than his back. This is important for it helps saliva, mucus, or vomitus flow more freely from the mouth.

2. Loosen any tight clothing around the neck.

3. Remove any hard or sharp objects near the victim so he cannot hurt himself.

4. If possible, place a thick wad of cloth such as a towel (or a folded leather belt, leather wallet, or leather glove) between the patient's teeth on the side of the mouth to protect him from biting his tongue or breaking a tooth.

5. False teeth should be removed after or between convulsions. Be careful not to be bitten yourself.

6. Extend the victim's chin so that his head is bent backward and the jaw forward to aid breathing.

7. Call your doctor—especially if the convulsions do not stop by themselves within fifteen minutes, or if unconsciousness lasts longer than ten minutes after convulsions have stopped.

8. A person who is a known epileptic may be carrying or wearing identification to that effect. Check to see and inform the physician accordingly.

9. Be calm and reassuring, particularly after the attack, as this will ease the patient's own fears and feelings of embarrassment.

10. Any attack of convulsions, regardless of the length of the episode, should be reported to the patient's doctor.

What NOT to Do

1. Do not attempt to pour liquids into the victim's mouth or throw water on his face.

2. Do not force anything hard between the teeth.

3. Do not attempt to stop the convulsions by holding the victim still or slapping or shaking him.

4. Do not be worried if a person who is a known epileptic is semistuporous, unresponsive, or extremely restless, talks incoherently, or seems confused for a period of time following the attack. This is the usual reaction during the recovery period.

— 33 —

STROKE

A stroke is a sudden weakness or paralysis most frequently affecting one side of the body, often affecting speech, and usually accompanied by loss of consciousness. It is due to an interruption of the blood supply to an area of the brain.

High blood pressure and hardening of the arteries are the most frequent underlying factors. Therefore, strokes tend to occur most commonly in older people.

Most strokes are not fatal. In fact, there are more than two million people living in the United States today who have had a stroke. With the best current methods of treatment, 90 per cent of the victims paralyzed by stroke will be able to walk again and to take care of themselves. Programs for complete rehabilitation of stroke patients are increasing in hospitals and clinics throughout the country.

Symptoms

Symptoms vary markedly depending upon the severity and the location of the damage to the brain. They may be:

Headache

Weakness or paralysis of a single arm or leg

Weakness or paralysis of an arm and leg on the same side of the body

Drooping of one side of the face

171

Difficulty in speaking
Nausea and vomiting
Dizziness, drowsiness, unconsciousness, or deep coma

What to Do

1. If a stroke is suspected, call your doctor immediately.

2. The patient should be placed in bed or kept flat.

3. If he is having difficulty breathing, he should be turned on his side to allow secretions to flow easily from his mouth.

4. Since he may have difficulty in swallowing, do not attempt to give any fluids or food or medicines.

5. If breathing has stopped or is extremely labored or noisy, begin mouth-to-mouth breathing (pp. 26-29) and continue until breathing is spontaneous and unlabored—or until medical assistance arrives.

Part Five

OTHER POTENTIALLY SERIOUS PROBLEMS

EYE PROBLEMS

FOREIGN BODIES IN THE EYE

Foreign bodies are the most common cause of eye injuries and a most frequent cause of impairment of vision, if proper treatment is not promptly carried out.

What to Do

If you can see the foreign body, try to dislodge it lightly with a moistened sterilized cotton swab or the moistened corner of a handkerchief. If the object cannot be removed after two or three attempts—or if it cannot be seen—take the person to a doctor or hospital emergency room.

Never rub the eye, as this may force the object to penetrate the eye still deeper.

CHEMICAL BURNS OF THE EYE

Many chemicals can cause serious damage when they come in contact with the eye. Speed is of the utmost importance in lessening the extent of the injury.

What to Do

1. **Immediately** wash the eyes with a gentle stream of cold running water poured from a cup or glass or from the hand. Keep irrigating until you are sure the chemical has been completely removed.

2. Cover the injured eye (or eyes) with a dry, sterile gauze pad or the cleanest available cloth material (such

as part of a sheet or shirt or a freshly ironed hand-kerchief).

3. Call for a doctor right away.

4. Until the doctor comes, do not use oil, ointments, or any other chemicals, as they may increase the severity of the injury.

When You Should Call a Doctor Right Away About Your Eyes

1. If you receive a "black eye."

2. If you have pain in the eyes, over the eyes, or in the back of the head.

3. If you see halos around light.

4. If you are aware of a sudden worsening or blurring of vision.

5. If you are aware of double vision.

6. If you see better when wearing dark glasses or when in a dimly lit room, or if you do not see so well in a brightly lit room.

7. If there is a magenta red band which shows up on the white of the eye around the iris (the colored part).

8. If the whites of the eyes are red and the redness is not readily explained by recent alcoholic intake, sleepless fatigue, sunburn, or windburn.

9. If there is a discharge, or if there is sticky matter coming from the eyes or crusting of the lids.

— 35 —

EAR PROBLEMS

FOREIGN BODIES IN THE EAR

Insects, pebbles, stones, and seeds can become lodged in the external canal of the ear. Insects can frequently be induced to crawl back out of the ear canal if you hold a bright light close to the ear.

Do not put anything in the ear—such as a cotton swab, hairpin, paper clip, or fingernail—in an effort to remove the object. Nor is it a good idea to try to wash out the object yourself with oil or water. You should call your doctor as he can easily and safely remove it.

EARACHE

There are numerous causes for earaches of short duration, such as getting water in the ear or a sudden change of altitude aboard an airplane. If the earache occurs during a flight, you may be able to relieve the pain by frequent yawning and chewing gum.

However, any earache which persists for an hour or two without decreasing in intensity warrants a call to the doctor. Do not put anything in the ear such as a cotton swab, hairpin, paper clip, fingernail, or any ointment or drops. Any of these might do harm or interfere with the doctor's examination of the ear canal.

Until the doctor arrives:

What to Do

1. Apply a hot water bottle or electric heating pad to the ear.

2. Chew gum.

3. Use nose drops in the **nose**, which sometimes helps to open a clogged ear. Be sure the nose drops you use were previously prescribed for you by your doctor when you had a cold.

4. Take aspirin or any pain reliever prescribed for you in the past.

When You Should Call a Doctor About Your Ears

1. If your hearing is impaired.

2. If you have pain coming from the ear.

3. If you have a feeling of fullness in the ear.

4. If you are dizzy.

5. If you have ringing in the ears or strange sounds such as buzzing, thumping, roaring, or whistling.

6. If you have a discharge coming from your ear.

— 36 —

SORE THROATS

Most sore throats are part of the "common cold" or are symptoms of throat infections that have no serious significance. However, a sore throat can also be an early sign of such diseases as tonsillitis, scarlet fever, trench mouth, mononucleosis (glandular fever), diphtheria, and many others. A sore throat is not an emergency—except potentially in anyone who has not received immunization against diphtheria.

What to Do

1. Take and record your temperature and pulse (pp. 35-36).

2. See if you have a rash anywhere on your body.

3. Look down your throat to see if it is red or if there are patches of white or yellow.

4. Report any sore throat to your doctor, unless it is typical of the kind of sore throats you get with your usual cold.

5. Report any sore throat to your doctor if you have a history of rheumatic fever or a rheumatic heart condition—or if a sore throat persists beyond four or five days.

6. Do **not** take any antibiotics, unless specifically instructed by your doctor.

7. If the pain is severe, take aspirin or a pain reliever previously prescribed for you by your physician.

8. Gargle for five minutes every hour with a solution of one teaspoon of ordinary table salt to one half glass of water as hot as you can stand it.

179

— 37 —

FEVER AND CHILLS

Fever is body temperature above the normal range. Normal body temperature can vary from 97 degrees to over 99 degrees by mouth, and from 98 degrees to slightly above 100 degrees rectally (rectal temperature being approximately one whole degree higher than mouth temperature).

Sometimes chills precede a fever. If chills are not followed by fever within two hours, they are probably insignificant. Fever may be accompanied by headache, back and muscle aches, fatigue, weakness, and loss of appetite.

Fever should be regarded as an important sign of illness. It serves as one of the body's ways of fighting off infection. While producing discomfort, it is rarely harmful in itself. However, temperatures 104 degrees and above in infants and young children can result in convulsions, and temperatures 105 degrees and above in adults can be hazardous.

What to Do

1. Have the patient get into bed.

2. Take and record his temperature and pulse (pp. 35-36).

3. Call your doctor.

4. Until he comes, try to reduce high fever by giving aspirin (to a child under one year of age, give one baby aspirin—between the ages of one and five, give two baby aspirins).

5. Give the patient a sponge bath with cool water or rubbing alcohol.

6. Take and record his temperature every half hour until repeated sponging has reduced the fever.

SUDDEN ALLERGIC REACTIONS

Allergy is an abnormal tissue reaction to normally harmless or non-toxic substances. It can vary from mild skin itching following the application of cosmetics, for example, to the sneezing and runny nose of hay fever, to the itching of hives, and to the breathing distress of asthma.

Asthma requires medical treatment, and only quiet reassurance can be offered by any non-medical person. The severest form of hives (angioneurotic edema) is capable of causing such swelling at the base of the tongue that breathing is seriously interfered with.

While there are many causes of hives, the commonest include food (such as shellfish, nuts, fresh fruit), medicines taken by mouth or injected, insect stings, plant pollens, and dust. Emotional factors in themselves can be the sole cause of, or can contribute to, severe allergic reactions, especially hives.

What to Do for Hives

1. If there is tingling, itching, or swelling of the lips, tongue, or the inside of the mouth, call your doctor at once.

2. Do not take any more food or drink (except water) until the hives have subsided or until you have obtained your doctor's advice.

3. If you have an antihistamine (a hay fever remedy) available, take one immediately. Take no other medications until you have obtained further advice from your doctor.

4. Do **not** take a hot bath or hot shower, as heat tends to aggravate the itching and swelling of the skin.

– 39 –

EMERGENCIES IN PREGNANCY

EMERGENCY CHILDBIRTH

Childbirth is both natural and normal. Healthy babies have been born without assistance throughout the centuries. So if you find yourself in the emergency situation of helping a mother deliver her baby, be calm and let nature take its course. Don't worry if the baby comes rapidly—a speedy birth usually puts the least amount of strain on the emerging infant and the mother as well.

If you **are** the expectant mother, get someone to stay with you until the doctor comes and have the person do the following:

What to Do

1. Make sure the doctor or an ambulance has been called.

2. See that the mother lies down, preferably in bed.

3. Wash your hands and keep surroundings as clean as possible. Slip a clean towel under the mother's hips for the baby to come on to.

4. Be patient. If you feel there is time, boil a pair of scissors for five minutes as it will be used later to cut the cord.

5. Hold the baby gently as it emerges. Do not pull on the baby at any time.

6. When the baby has been delivered, hold the baby upside down by its feet. If it does not cry, slap it on the back a few times.

7. Use a clean handkerchief over your finger to clear the baby's mouth and throat of mucus.

8. If the baby still is not breathing, use very gentle mouth-to-mouth breathing (pp. 23-26) until it does.

9. After it has cried, place the baby on one side of the mother's abdomen face down with its head slightly lowered. Cover the baby to keep it warm.

10. Once the baby is securely breathing, wait for the afterbirth to be expelled. **Do not pull on the cord.**

11. If you did not have time before, boil a pair of scissors for five minutes or clean with alcohol.

12. If the doctor is on his way, wait for him to tie and cut the cord, as there is no rush about doing this. If no help is on the way, tie a clean handkerchief strip or shoelace firmly in a square knot around the umbilical cord about four inches from the baby to stop the circulation in the cord. Tie a second piece of material in a square knot around the cord six to eight inches from the baby (two to four inches beyond the first knot).

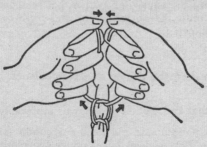

In tightening each loop of the square knot, avoid tugging on the umbilical cord. Steady one hand against the other at the knuckles as you pull the knot.

13. Cut the cord **between the two ties** with the clean scissors.

14. If the afterbirth has been only partially expelled, you may help push it out by pressing on the mother's uterus (a firm lump below the navel) with one hand.

15. Once the afterbirth has been completely expelled, gently massage the mother's abdomen to help her uterus contract (to minimize bleeding).

16. Keep the mother comfortable and see that the baby is warm and breathing.

17. Keep people away from both the baby and mother.

18. Handle the baby gently and as little as possible.

What NOT to Do

1. Do not try to hurry the birth.

2. Do not interfere with the birth in any way.

3. Do not hurry to cut the cord. You may even wait until the afterbirth has been completely expelled.

4. Do not wash the white material off the baby, as it protects the baby's skin.

5. Do nothing to the baby's eyes, ears, nose, or mouth.

Symptoms Indicating Potential Complications of PREGNANCY

If you develop any of the following symptoms, **call your doctor immediately.** Depending on the circumstances, he will then decide whether or not they are danger signals and will give you further instructions.

1. Vaginal bleeding*, no matter how slight
2. Sharp or continuous pain in the abdomen
3. Chills or fever
4. Persistent vomiting
5. Swelling of the face or fingers
6. Severe, persistent headache
7. Dimness or blurring of vision
8. Sudden escape of fluid from the vagina
9. A weight gain of several pounds in one week
10. Pain or burning on urination

*Go to bed at once and take nothing by mouth except water.

— 40 —

BOILS

A boil is the common term given to a localized infection of the skin. Such an infection may be situated around the base of a hair follicle and is called a furuncle. If the infection spreads and involves several hair follicles, it is referred to as a carbuncle. Common locations for either type of boil are: the back of the neck, the armpits, the buttocks, face, ear, nose, and extremities (arms and legs).

The occurrence of boils may be a clue to faulty skin hygiene, exposure to other individuals who harbor staphylococci (the person himself may have become a "staph" carrier), or the presence of diabetes. Boils in the known diabetic can be more serious.

What to Do

1. Do not squeeze a boil or pimple, as this may spread the infection. It may even lead to blood poisoning (septicemia) and abscesses deep within the body.

2. Keep the affected area free from pressure, friction, irritation, and unnecessary movement.

3. Any infections around the upper lip, nose, or near the eyes require medical advice, because of the danger of nervous system complications.

4. You may hasten the healing of a boil elsewhere by applying a hot, moist washcloth as frequently and as long as possible.

5. If a boil should begin to drain, wipe the discharge off with sterile or clean gauze or cotton soaked with rubbing alcohol. Then cover the area with a sterile adhesive bandage strip.

6. Do not attempt to open or lance a boil yourself.

7. Call your doctor if a boil fails to heal rapidly, or if it becomes larger or more painful, or if you see red streaks traveling up the arm or leg.

— 41 —

POISON IVY, POISON OAK,
POISON SUMAC

Two thirds of all people who touch poison ivy develop a skin rash. The severity of the rash depends upon the amount and area of contact and the person's individual sensitivity.

Poison oak and poison sumac are less frequent offenders but give the same symptoms as poison ivy to the sensitive person. In addition to direct contact, smoke from burning leaves of all three plants can cause a rash. In all cases, the rash is accompanied by itching, and frequently small blisters develop.

The symptoms, which are actually allergic reactions, may develop within a few hours after exposure but may also be delayed for as long as a week or more. The rash produced by any of these poisonous plants is not contagious. It cannot be spread from one person to another.

Prevention

A rash may be prevented or minimized by thoroughly washing the exposed skin with mild soap and water, if it is done within half an hour to an hour after exposure. Lather and rinse several times and sponge the area with rubbing alcohol, if available.

Clothing may pick up and retain the oily poison upon contact with the plant or with the contaminated skin. Be sure to wash contaminated clothing and allow it to hang for several days before wearing it again.

The best prevention is **avoidance of contact.** You must know how to recognize these poisonous plants. Wear protective clothing when necessary.

POISON IVY

POISON OAK

POISON SUMAC

What to Do

For mild eruptions use a calamine lotion to minimize the itching or cold compresses of Burow's solution (diluted one part to twenty with water) to minimize soreness. The most important thing is to try to avoid scratching, as this may spread the rash or even cause it to become infected.

For severe or persistent eruptions, consult your doctor.

Part Six

PSYCHIATRIC EMERGENCIES

– 42 –

THREATENED SUICIDE

Five million Americans now alive have at one time or another tried to take their own lives. Every year twenty-five thousand succeed. Suicide is the ninth leading cause of death in the United States.

It has been said that most people who threaten suicide do not attempt to carry it out. This is a false and dangerous premise. Every threat of suicide should be taken seriously within the limits of common sense, for some people do use such threats almost every day of their lives as a matter of expression.

Suicidal attempts occur mainly in the following types of people (and situations):

1. A person who is in constant pain or **believes** he has an incurable illness.

2. A person who is depressed and hopeless, feels he is worthless, and loses interest in things that had previously interested him.

3. A person who is impulsive and tends not to think of the consequences of his acts—such a person is frequently an alcoholic.

4. A person, most commonly a young woman or an immature young man, who makes a suicidal attempt for dramatic impact and to serve some purpose.

Suicide is more often attempted by someone with a history of a previous suicide attempt, or a history of a "nervous breakdown." The development of bizarre or unusual behavior may be a warning sign. Unfortunately, many families make excuses and allowances for their members instead of seeking medical advice.

DEPRESSION

A suicidal threat is most ominous when it has been preceded by other changes in the personality indicative of depression. Depression is a relative term, as we all are depressed at certain times and to varying degrees.

The more serious depressions are manifested by continued expressions of fears, worthlessness, self-incrimination, inability to enjoy previous pleasures, inability to foresee anything good in the future, loss of interest in friends and daily events, periods of brooding, and such behavior changes as loss of appetite, withdrawal, sleeplessness, unusual irritability or agitation, excessive worry, preoccupation with bodily sensations and functions, and deterioration in normal habits of cleanliness, grooming, and dress. By no means do all these manifestations need to be present for a depression to be severe.

Remain with the Person

If you are concerned enough to call the doctor, do not leave such a person unattended for even a moment —even while you are making the call to the doctor. It is extremely rare that anyone, unless completely out of his mind, will make a suicidal attempt while attended by another person.

You need not be afraid to discuss the situation over the telephone in front of a person who is depressed. In fact, the realization that you are aware of the condition is sometimes quite reassuring to someone so despondent.

— 43 —

DANGEROUS OR VIOLENT

BEHAVIOR

While dangerous or violent behavior can come on suddenly without previous warning, it is more likely to follow a period of strange, angry, or threatening behavior. It may help to recognize that, since violent behavior is not condoned by society, the person exhibiting it is frequently mentally or physically ill. This type of behavior can also occur in mentally defective individuals.

Some common causes are: confused states resulting from fever, other medical illness, or medications; certain rare types of epilepsy; panic states; paranoid schizophrenic reactions; the manic phase of a manic-depressive illness. Alcoholism and recent or repeated head injuries may be entirely or partially responsible for aggressive or violent outbursts.

What to Do

1. Try not to become excited.

2. Do not try to argue, reason, restrain, or fight back with a person in this state.

3. Get away as quickly as possible, taking any children with you and warning any adults so they will follow you.

4. Call the police or your doctor as soon as you are safely away.

— 44 —

DISORIENTATION OR

MENTAL CONFUSION

Mental or physical illness or intoxication can cause a person to lose contact with reality in varying degrees, with accompanying changes in his appearance, speech, behavior, reasoning, and memory. For example, he may be dazed or confused as to who he is, who you are, where he is, what time, day, or year it is. Furthermore, he may be unaware of his confusion or disorientation and he may even be subject to hallucinations, illusions, or delusions. Delirium is a state of total confusion when there is no contact at all with reality.

Some common causes are: fever; alcoholic or other forms of intoxication; many kinds of medication in normal or excessive dosage; head injury; stroke; heart failure; pneumonia; uncontrolled diabetes; uremic (or kidney) poisoning. In addition, a state of confusion is common following a convulsion and may either precede or follow unconsciousness or coma.

What to Do

1. Call a doctor.

2. If possible, see that someone is in constant attendance, as the person may accidentally hurt himself. For example, he might fall out of bed or from a window— he might start a fire by smoking in bed.

3. Be calm and reassuring to the patient.

4. If the person is indoors, keep the room brightly lit, as darkness will only add to his confusion and fear.

5. If the person seems thirsty, help him to drink some water or a soft drink.

6. Do not give alcohol in any form or any medication.

7. Keep trying to explain to the person who he is, where he is, who you are, and what has happened to him.

8. Keep him as comfortable as possible until the doctor comes.

Part Seven

DENTAL EMERGENCIES

_____

— 45 —

TOOTH PAIN

Even though dentistry has come a long way since its beginnings in prerecorded history (Etruscan ruins in Italy have yielded gold dental bridges older than Greek medical texts), dental pain still remains one of the commonest and most dreaded afflictions of man.

The causes of the pain, which can vary from simple decay to a root abscess, must be diagnosed and treated by a dentist or oral surgeon. However, for those times when dental consultation is not immediately available, it is helpful to know how to alleviate the pain itself.

What to Do for Pain from a Cavity

1. If you can see a cavity in the aching tooth, rinse vigorously with tepid water to try to remove particles of food or decay.

2. If you have oil of cloves, saturate a small piece of cotton and gently place it next to or into the cavity.

3. Take two aspirins or a pain reliever previously prescribed for you by your physician.

4. Sit in a comfortable chair or, if it is nighttime, prop yourself up high in bed (lying down tends to increase the pain).

5. Try holding mouthfuls of ice water which brings relief in some instances.

6. Call your dentist.

What to Do for Pain from Loss of a Filling

1. Chew a piece of candlewax, beeswax, or paraffin along with some strands of sterile cotton.

2. Use this material to cover the jagged edges of the tooth to prevent cutting or irritating the tongue.

3. Call your dentist.

What to Do for a Broken Tooth

SAME AS FOR PAIN FROM LOSS OF A FILLING

What to Do for Pain from Dental Abscess or Infection

1. Take two aspirins or a pain reliever previously prescribed by your physician or dentist.

2. Find a position that is comfortable. You may want to sit in a chair or lie propped up in bed. You may find that lying down flat is the most comfortable position.

3. Apply an electric heating pad or hot water bottle to the painful side of the face.

4. Call your dentist or physician.

What to Do for Pain from Extraction or Injury

1. Take two aspirins or a pain reliever previously prescribed by your physician or dentist.

2. Apply an ice pack to the painful or injured side of the face.

3. Call your dentist or physician.

– 46 –

BLEEDING

Anyone who has had an extraction or other oral surgery is usually instructed before leaving the dentist's office or the hospital in how to stop heavy bleeding. However, bleeding may also occur after an injury and, on rare occasions, spontaneously.

There is no need to worry about swallowing small amounts of blood, but if possible, try to avoid swallowing large amounts of blood, which may result in nausea and vomiting.

What to Do

1. Make a small pack from sterile gauze or a clean cloth.

2. Place the pack directly over the bleeding point.

3. Bite or press down on it **firmly** for at least 30 minutes.

4. Apply an ice pack to that side of the face.

5. Call your dentist or oral surgeon.

6. Remain quiet. Sit up or lie propped up in bed.

7. Do not eat, drink, smoke, or rinse the mouth until the pack has been removed and the bleeding has stopped.

DISLOCATION OF THE LOWER JAW

The simple act of yawning can sometimes result in dislocation of the jaw, a condition in which the mouth is open and cannot be closed without first-aid or medical assistance. A dislocation may occur when the mouth is opened wide during dental work, or even at the dinner table.

There is usually time to take the victim of a dislocated jaw to a physician or dentist. In some cases, however, knowledge and use of the proper method of replacement can result in immediate relief of discomfort and disability.

What to Do

1. Place the victim in a chair.

2. Wrap a protective covering (such as a handkerchief or thickly folded gauze) several times around each of your thumbs before attempting to set the patient's dislocation.

3. Face the person.

4. Have the person take out any removable dentures or bridgework.

5. Place your thumbs as far back as you can over the lower molars on each side of the jaw (or where the molars would be if they are missing).

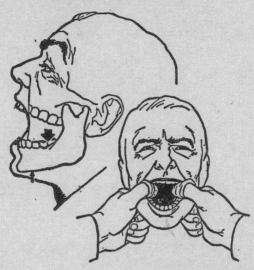

Drawing by Anthony Ravielli, from *The Complete Book of First Aid*, by John Henderson, M.D., published by Bantam Books, Inc. © Copyright 1955 by John Henderson. Reprinted by permission of Bantam Books.

6. With the fingers of each hand under the patient's chin, press down slowly and strongly with your thumbs.

7. As the back of the jaw starts to go down, guide it backwards. The person's chin will start to go up.

8. As the jaw begins to go back in place, slip your thumbs out of the way along the side of each jawbone to avoid their being painfully squeezed when the jaw snaps back into place.

9. To prevent the jaw from dislocating again, the patient should keep his mouth closed and not eat or chew.

10. The jaw should now be secured by a chin bandage made from a large handkerchief folded first into a triangle and then into a band about three inches wide. Draw it under the chin and tie it tightly on the top of the head.

11. Call your physician or dentist for further advice.

12. If the dislocation does not respond to the treatment just outlined after you have made two or three attempts, do not try further. Obtain professional help.

Part Eight

HOME EMERGENCY SUPPLIES

HOME EMERGENCY
SUPPLIES

Item	Quantity	Special Use
1. Thermometer, oral or rectal	1	
2. Ice bag	1	
3. Electric heating pad or hot water bottle	1	
4. Plastic sheeting or rubber sheeting or oilcloth	1 piece	For covering electric heating pads *not* designed for safe use next to wet surfaces
5. Eye cup	1	For rinsing eyes
6. Bandage scissors (with blunt tip)	1	For cutting bandages or clothing
7. Tweezers (with fine points)	1	For removing splinters and ticks
8. Measuring spoons, metal or plastic	1 set	
9. Flashlight and batteries	1 3	Keep batteries wrapped separately in moistureproof covering next to, but not inside, flashlight.

Item	Quantity	Special Use
10. Airway (or resuscitation) tube	2	For mouth-to-mouth breathing—one to keep at home, one to keep in the family car
11. Triangular bandages, 37" × 37" square, cut or folded diagonally, with two safety pins each	2	For arm slings
12. Sterile gauze pads in sealed envelopes, 2" × 2", 4" × 4", and 4" × 7"	12 of each size	
13. Plain sterile gauze in widths of 1", 2", and 3"	2 rolls each	
14. Adhesive tape in widths of ½", 1", and 2"	1 roll each	
15. Adhesive strip bandages	1 pack of assorted sizes	
16. Large sanitary napkins, individually wrapped	4	
17. Sanitary napkin belt	1	
18. Sterile cotton	1 1-lb. roll	
19. Cotton-tipped applicators	1 small box	
20. Wooden tongue blades	12	For splinting broken fingers
21. Mild soap	1 bar	

Item	Quantity	Special Use
22. Tincture of green soap	1 small (4-oz.) bottle	For dog and cat bites
23. Rubbing alcohol	1 bottle	
24. Household (3 per cent) hydrogen peroxide	1 small (4-oz.) bottle,	
25. Bland eyedrops	1 dropper bottle, ½-1 oz.	
26. Aspirin for adults and children	1 bottle each	
27. Petroleum jelly	1 small tube or jar	
28. Glycerin suppositories and	Box of 12	For hard stool in the rectum
29. Rubber finger cots	1 small box	
30. Calamine lotion or Burow's solution	1 8-oz. bottle	For poison ivy, poison oak, poison sumac
31. Ipecac syrup or activated charcoal	1 1-oz. bottle 1 small box	For use in household chemical poisoning
32. Cornstarch or flour	1 small box	To induce vomiting in iodine poisoning
33. Table salt and	1 small box	For shock
34. Baking soda (or bicarbonate of soda)	1 8-oz. box	
35. Household ammonia (or baking soda)	1 small bottle	For insect stings
36. Cold cream or shortening or salad oil	1 small container	For sunburn

Item	Quantity	Special Use
37. Mineral oil or salad oil or machine oil	1 small container	For removal of ticks

It is advisable to put small amounts of the common household items (no. 32 through no. 37) in well-marked containers and store with the rest of your emergency supplies so they are *always* on hand.

The following can be obtained only with your doctor's prescription and, of course, are subject to his approval:

38. A strong pain reliever

39. A sedative

40. An antihistamine (hay fever remedy) for sudden and severe allergic reactions

▲KEEP EMERGENCY SUPPLIES FRESH AND CLEAN

▲CLEAN OUT YOUR MEDICINE CABINETS REGULARLY— DISCARD PRESCRIPTIONS NO LONGER NEEDED

▲KEEP ALL MEDICINES AND HOUSEHOLD CHEMICALS

1) OUT OF THE REACH OF CHILDREN

2) PROPERLY LABELED

3) RETURNED TO THEIR STORAGE PLACE **immediately** AFTER USE

INDEX

MOUTH-TO-MOUTH BREATHING

1. Place victim on back immediately. Turn head to one side and quickly **clear mouth and throat** of mucus, food, or other obstruction.

2. **Tilt head back** as far as possible, stretching neck.

3. Open mouth, place thumb in corner of mouth.

4. **Pinch nostrils, open your mouth wide, and blow until chest rises.**
For an adult: REPEAT 10 TO 15 TIMES A MINUTE (every 5 or 6 seconds) blowing vigorously.
For a child: REPEAT 20 TIMES A MINUTE (every 3 seconds) taking shallow breaths.

5. **For an infant,** seal both mouth and nose with your mouth and blow gently with small puffs of air from your cheeks. REPEAT 20 TIMES A MINUTE (every 3 seconds).

6. If you wish, you can cover victim's nose and mouth with handkerchief or cloth to avoid direct contact. Rescue breathing still works well.

IMPORTANT PERSONAL NOTES

NAME _____

BLOOD TYPE _____

ALLERGIES _____

_____

DATE OF LAST SMALLPOX VACCINATION _____

DATE OF LAST TETANUS VACCINATION _____

NAME _____

BLOOD TYPE _____

ALLERGIES _____

_____

DATE OF LAST SMALLPOX VACCINATION _____

DATE OF LAST TETANUS VACCINATION _____

NAME _____

BLOOD TYPE _____

ALLERGIES _____

_____

DATE OF LAST SMALLPOX VACCINATION _____

DATE OF LAST TETANUS VACCINATION _____

NAME _____

BLOOD TYPE _____

ALLERGIES _____

_____

DATE OF LAST SMALLPOX VACCINATION _____

DATE OF LAST TETANUS VACCINATION _____

PYRAMID
BOOKS